They Came for Coffee

A Story of Finnish Fortitude, Love, and Coffee

By
Elaine Lillback

© 2014 Elaine Lillback
ISBN: 978-1-312-79431-3

About the Author

Elaine Tikka Lillback was born in Perry, Ohio graduating from Perry Schools. She attended Ohio State University, receiving her baccalaureate from Judson College in Chicago, Illinois. She has a Masters degree in Elementary Education from Kent State University. She taught in both private and public schools. Her late husband, Eugene, was a math professor at Kent State University. She has traveled extensively overseas and has served as a missionary teacher in Canada and Central Africa. Elaine and Eugene have three sons and she is proud of her several grandchildren and great grandchildren. She has written extensively on the Finnish experience in America. Her published books include: *Finn Hollow of Fairport, Ohio, Lempi of Finn Hollow*, and *John Morton: Forgotten Founding Father*. She has also translated Charles Potti's Finnish novel *Elma* into English. She was inducted into the Perry High School Hall of Fame and into the Finnish Heritage Museum in Fairport, Ohio Hall of Fame. Along with writing, painting has been one of her favorite hobbies.

Photos of Elaine as a young girl.

-1-
It Begins with Coffee

That aroma, that fantastic, alluring fragrance! What was it? It enhanced the air. What could it be? Somewhere in the world someone had plucked the red cherry-like berries growing on a shimmering green bush, tasted them, and found the taste to be invigorating. Dropping the berries in a fire pit, the roasted berries called for further tasting in a not so pure water supply. But, ah-ha! It tasted different-- good! And the taste for coffee was born.

Coffee berries in Bali. Photo credit: Jean-Marie Hullot

As people traveled from place to place, coffee was shared and refined. How many tales of friendship, created by sharing a cup of coffee, could be garnered from over the centuries of time? However, our story is not about coffee, but about the touching, warming, and unknown binding influence coffee has been for the Finnish people, bringing them together over the course of time.

Our story takes us from the early twentieth century in Finland and on to America where we meet with Finns around the Finnish coffee table. Whenever two people sat down to talk together, there was a steaming coffee kettle near at hand waiting to be poured out as a gesture of friendship. These were often times of fun and laughter and strength in sharing trials and the giving of mutual encouragement.

-2-
The Hope of a New Land

Life in Finland had been difficult for centuries. Tennant farming barely gave the Finns their daily bread. Very little money was earned by their long, excruciating hours of labor as they served the overseeing lords under either the Swedish or Russian rule. The land was beautiful with its rocks and flowing hills which wrapped around bubbling streams and shimmering lakes. However, earning a living was continuously hard in the late nineteenth and early twentieth century as the people strived for land ownership and independence. The charms of nature and the love of the land did not make life easier; it was still primitive and hard. So it was during those farming generations that a few adventurous, inquisitive folks in every village had the itch of curiosity motivating them to ponder how life and coffee tasted on the other side of the big waters-- in the new world, America.

Coffee beans had come to Finland by traders who had sailed from the coasts of far-away places. Finns began roasting the beans and grinding them in their homes, amplifying coffee's importance for families and their circle of friendships. Through coffee, not only were the cultural values of the land mellowed, but the Finns, both the rich and poor, were prompted to investigate and explore more of world interests.

Due to their curiosity, many Finnish ancestors came to America seeking a better life. Often it was a harder life, but it offered the promise of getting ahead. There was the hope of succeeding from a tenant farmer in Finland to becoming the owner of one's own home in the new land. They could become respected citizens in a new land. Those who had immigrated before and had found life and work to be satisfactory encouraged their families and friends in Finland to come and join them in the new world. When those interested were ready to leave the homeland, the travel expenses of their family or friends were advanced to them. These monies were to be paid later as a loan.

Young single men and women as well as married men, who left their wives and family to wait for traveling funds, came to find work through various means. The women often served as maids in the homes of wealthy magnates and officials. There they gained great acceptability because of their dedication in providing meticulous care in food preparation and household chores. Men, strong and courageous, were willing to engage in dangerous, gut-wrenching labor as they developed railroad beds, emptied ship's cargoes of coal or iron ore, or as miners of coal, iron, and other rich minerals from the belly of American soil. It was an opportunity for the immigrants to grow wealthier in the new world. New surroundings with new friends and many new jobs were developed, but new ideas were usually introduced when sharing a cup of coffee around a friend's family coffee table.

-3-
The Finn's Love of Coffee

A traditional tea service set

The taste for coffee seems to be genetically passed along for the Finns, almost literally handed from grandmother to grandchild as observed in the following account.

Little two-year-old Elspeth was sitting on her grandmother Kendra's lap as grandma was enjoying her morning cup of coffee. To satisfy the child's curiosity regarding the coffee, Kendra dipped her finger in the coffee and placed it in the child's mouth saying, "Coffee, it tastes bitter. It's not for children."

Tasting it, the child smacked her lips and responded, "Mmmm, coffee," and then stuck her thumb in the cup testing the strange liquid again. The grandmother laughed, "Coffee, yes. It is kahvia, Finnish kahvia." With that, Elspeth quickly dipped her thumb once again, tasted, and said, "Kahvia, it's good!"

The identifying story of Finnish-Americans is the story of the shared cup of coffee, "the kuppi kahvia." The Finns love of sharing tales, songs, proverbs, riddles, and things of deep thought made for happy conversation. Sometimes this lent itself to a disposition of satire, revealing their own or other's erroneous ways and experiences. Coffee talk often became the time of personal problem solving and encouragement.

-4-
Senja's Childhood

During the warm, long summer nights of 1922 in central Finland, the youth of the Alajarvi area would gather together for evenings of fun and dancing. Senja, with heaviness in her heart, had joined the group. Life had not been easy for her. Both of her parents, Alexander and Johanna Korhea-Aho Hautala, had died during Senja's early childhood. She and her surviving siblings, three brothers and a sister, Aune, were now growing up as orphans on the Hannula uncles' farm.

The father had been by nature a horse trader, but he began buying and trading properties. Charitably, Alexander had tried to help those neighbors who were in danger of losing their homes by buying properties. However, he died at the early age of forty-four on February 10, 1914. Before that time, he had bought and sold their family home four different times. Each time he took on legally the new family name with the purchased property as Finnish law required. According to law, the family name went with the farm to become the name of the new owner. The family names had been: Hautala, Lindbacka, and Korhea-Aho. At the end of the last trade he had returned the family back to their original home, taking the name Hautala once again.

After Alexander's death, Senja's mother, Johanna, was left alone with five children. She had previously lost five other children during their early childhood. One baby girl died before Senja's birth on December 29, 1895. The four others were born and died during Senja's first twelve years of life. Brother Reino was born two months after Senja's twelfth birthday. When Reino was nine in 1917, Johanna died leaving the children orphaned. Senja became the head of the family along with nine-year-old Reino. Fortunately, their father's relatives soon recognized that the difficult load of caring for her siblings was too great for Senja.

As the oldest child, now in her twenties, Senja knit the orphaned group together, making the home comfortable for her three siblings. They now lived at the spacious home of Uncles Nikolai, Hemminki, and Matti Hannula in Ojajarvi, Finland. The uncles assumed the care of all of their brother Alexander's children. However, three-year-old Toivo was reared by another prosperous, childless family.

Uncle Nikolai Hannula was a gracious, intelligent man and provided well for the orphaned children. His farm with the big red house and barn overlooked the grassy hillside above Lake Ojajarvi. It was a happy place for the children to grow.

-5-
Two Proposals

Not far away in an adjoining village of Luoma-Aho, there lived a prosperous, older man who was the village tailor. Concerned about Senja's fast disappearing courting years, Uncle Nikolai made plans for Senja to be wed to this tailor. Although this was done according to custom, Senja had not been asked if this was acceptable with her. When she was finally consulted about her uncle's plans, she excitedly said, "I don't even know the man!"

The tailor, however, was happy with the selection, and soon their betrothal was set to be announced according to church protocol for the next three consecutive Sundays. If there was no reason to hinder the marriage, they would be wed within a few weeks. Senja would become the wife of the respected, but unknown to her, village tailor. The first of the three Sundays for the church announcement was to be in a week!

No matter how much chicory-type coffee she drank, she worried. Was this the way her life would be? She had been considering how her future would change. How could she marry someone she didn't even know? She only knew the tailor as her uncle's friend. He did have a lovely yellow house. He would provide a good life and she would be respected in the village. She could hope to have her own children. She'd had a lot of childhood experience caring for her little siblings.

Complicating matters further, a few weeks earlier, she had received a letter from a young Finn-American, Richard Lillback. He'd learned about Senja and gotten her address from her Grandmother Wilhelmina Lillstrang in Fairport Harbor, Ohio. Encouraged to write to her, he identified himself as the stepson of Senja's Aunt

The Lillstrang Home on Sixth Street. From left to right: Isaac and Hulda Lillback, Anna Lillstrang, Wilhelmina Lillstrang and Jacob Lillstrang. The five Lillstrang children are: Rudolph, Fredolph, Ruth, Delores, and baby Whitey.

Hulda. Aunt Hulda was the daughter of Wilhelmina and the wife of Richard's father, Isaac. Hulda was also Senja's mother's sister.

Hulda, Isaac, and Rudolph Lillback. Isaac was Richard's father and Hulda was Senja's aunt and Richard's stepmother.

Reino, seeing Senja reading her letter over and over again, queried, "Now what's that letter all about? Why do you keep reading it? Is it about something we should tell Uncle?"

"Oh Reino, I think so. Look at this picture. This young, handsome man, Richard Lillback, not only sent his picture to me, but money for a ticket to New York City in America. He says, just like that, 'Will you come to America and marry me?' He writes he was born in Hanhikoski, Finland. His father, Isaac Richard Lillback III, had gone to America to work and was waiting for his family to join him. But Richard was five when his mother died in Finland of pneumonia as she prepared to go to America. Richard was sent to live with his grandfather, Isaac Lillback II, five miles away from here in Untamala. He grew up there. At the age of eighteen, he received money from his father for a ticket to Fairport, Ohio. Now he writes, 'I have a job and my own home here in Fairport. It's near your Grandmother Wilhelmina, and your Aunt Hulda. They have told me about you. Will you come and join me in marriage? I'm sending you passage money.'"

-6-
A Difficult Decision

"I wish I'd known about all this a long time ago," Senja thought, shaking her head. "This is my whole life, and now I have to decide in a few hours what to do."

Senja sought advice from her brother, "Reino, a week from tomorrow morning the wedding announcement is to be heard at church for the first time. Uncle has arranged that I'll be married to the tailor from Luoma-Aho. Then there'll be two more of these announcements on the Sundays before the marriage happens. What should I do? I don't know this man or that American fellow!"

Reino chuckled, "Looks like you're going to get married pretty soon! You better talk to Uncle and do what you think is best for you. Here comes Aunt and Uncle now you'd better tell them."

Soothed by Reino's positive attitude toward her opportunity to go to America, Senja seized the precarious moment and began nervously to tell Uncle of her marriage proposal from America.

"Oh Uncle, can this be? I would be near grandmother and Aunt Hulda. Is it possible? Oh, how can I take care of the arrangement with the tailor?" Senja inquired. "Could I go to America, and perhaps marry a young man? Oh! Uncle."

"GO!" exclaimed her aunt who was listening. "A young girl needs a younger man. You need to get to Vaasa and get a passport right away on Monday."

"Senja, I do believe the young man's proposal is God's plan for you. We were trying to make your life, but God has a better plan, it seems," mused Uncle. "We'll go ahead and seek the passport from Vaasa. It'll be necessary to quietly go about this and see how God provides for you. We have three weeks to get you to Helsinki. Reino, keep this information under your cap, and let's watch God work."

"I'm going to the winter night's festival at the church youth center, now" responded Reino. "Are you coming with me, Senja? Come on and clear your head, and have some fun!"

-7-

Preparing for Vaasa

As the youth intermingled at the church, they laughed and enjoyed the indoor fun. Senja however, was silently formulating a quick life-changing plan. In her twenties, she was old enough. Tomorrow she'd leave for Vaasa and get the passport. She would not be in church on Sunday! She had the money to go to America, but did she have the courage and stamina? After all, she didn't speak English. Well, she was going to Vaasa to see if she could get a passport to America anyway!

It was a secret and she couldn't tell any of her friends! Trying to be secretive was hard; she wanted to shout it out! Returning home from church, she was almost flying as she skied through January's fresh fallen snow. What would she pack in her duffle bag and her straw suitcase? She had only a few dresses, but she'd take her Sunday best. There was probably an early train leaving the next morning; she had to leave before she was forced to change her mind. Uncle would probably see her to the station. She had to go downstairs to present her plan to the family this very moment!

Explaining her pent up feelings was not difficult after she had read Richard's letter to the family. They did understand her desire to meet with the young man in America. She had had so many responsibilities in her life; she would get along all right even with the stresses of a new land and new home.

Saying goodbye to her family to make the trip to Vaasa was not easy, and she did not dare to think of how the tailor would feel when she did not show up for the church announcement! Uncle would have a lot of explaining to do. He was the one that hatched the plan and now he would have to concentrate on its nullification. However, he had better wait until everything was worked out for Senja's departure to America.

Senja tried not to worry about that. All she could think of was how life was changing. There certainly was adventure ahead. She had not dared to dream of going to shining America; it was now a new world of her own. Those thoughts rang loudly in her heart like the American Liberty Bell she had heard about.

"What if you don't like Richard?" asked sister Aune.

"If I don't like Richard, I'll get a job in America, and pay him back the passage money! I have to go to America; I can't marry this elderly man I don't even know! God help me!" cried Senja.

"What will all your friends say when they hear you're gone?" asked Reino.

"Tell them I'm writing a new Hautala history, and they're to come see me in America. I'll serve them real coffee, not chickory! And, oh, thank you Uncle. I do appreciate the love and care that you've given all of us. May God bless you all! Forgive me for changing your plans for me. I do love all of you, Auntie and Uncle Nikolai and Hemminki and Matti. Perhaps you can come to see me in America."

There wasn't much sleeping at the Hannula's that night, and Senja was off early for Vaasa on the morning train. There were many things to do. She had to get medical papers and a travel permit. She had the money for the ticket in Helsinki, but now she would need money for the passport, the health shots and papers. Uncle slipped an envelope of money and a lunch in her duffle bag.

-8-
The Beginning of an Adventure

It was January 14, 1922 when Senja arrived in Vaasa, applying for her passport to America. It was a new experience. Several days were required for them to check her church credentials. A picture was needed for identification. Her serious demeanor was photographed and attached to her passport. For 150 Finnmarks, she now had her passport to take her to America. It was stamped and signed for another 16 Finnmarks. She carefully placed it in her bag and returned to the railroad station and headed for home.

She needed to decide on clothing to take while getting her minimal things in order. In a week she would be leaving home and going to Helsinki to board a local ship to carry her to England. There, she would need to allow plenty of time for purchasing her ticket and completing whatever was demanded by the American consulate for her passage. The excitement of the new experience was making her nervous.

Being at home for the week was helpful in settling her nerves. It gave Senja ample time to talk with her aunt and uncle about travel and about how life in America might be. They had heard many stories over the years from some of their family and friends who had ventured to the new world. Uncle Nikolai had not canceled the betrothal yet; he was waiting for her departure before he met with the bridegroom tailor. It appeared he was a little nervous, too. He was beginning to realize that sometimes his plans were not always the best. Being older was not always wiser. Even wise King Solomon had learned that.

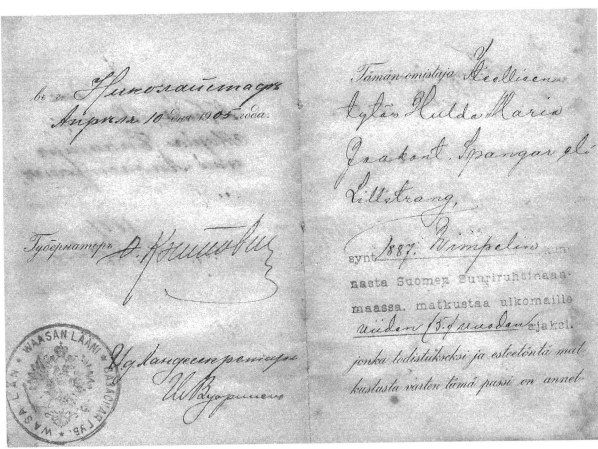

A Finnish Passport. This is a page from Senja's Aunt Hulda's passport.

Helsinki, the Departure Site

Downtown Helsinki in the 1920s

It was early February 1922. The journey by train carried Senja over the snowy countryside through central Finland to Helsinki. She contemplated her hasty departure. She had sometimes rehearsed such a thing in her mind, hoping that someday she might be able to do what many of Finland's youth had been doing: going to America to find their pot of gold. Now she was traveling in a known direction to a somewhat unknown future without a human guide or guidebook. She was putting her trust in God who had always been her strength during those difficult and trying years of her childhood and youth.

She knew there were things she would have to take care of in Helsinki. There had to be some medical shots and the acquiring of a certified health permit. She already had the Finnish passport which would enable her to travel overseas to England and beyond. She considered herself strong and healthy; hopefully she would not be deterred now or when she arrived at Ellis Island in New York City. She had heard many stories of those who had failed to pass the health exam and had to return home defeated in their quest.

Helsinki, one of the southernmost cities in Finland, was on the Gulf of Finland. It was one of the most appropriate ports from which travelers could leave for Liverpool, England. It had ice-breaker ships that could run the harbor for most of the winter. There were hotels where a room could be obtained until the ship and the necessary papers were ready for the traveler. The young men and women would become acquainted with each other as they waited for departure. They were advised that sometimes the wait lasted many days. They all seemed to be headed for America, and as they talked together, they spun their dreams of life in that new land. New York was the city they talked about. But first, they had to get to Hull, England. Then it was on to Liverpool where they would board the ocean liner S.S. Cameronia. It was scheduled to arrive in New York on March 8, 1922.

The conversations flowed in their native Finnish language, although some spoke in different dialects as the travelers represented various provinces of Finland. It was fun listening to the conversations. Senja participated in the ongoing chatter but became worried about the difficulties presented when she would arrive in America without knowing any English. Fortunately, there were Finns where she was going in Fairport, Ohio. But she needed to have providential assistance to get through the hard places in England and New York.

Voyage to a New Land

Senja's travel funds were limited. She had a small amount of Finnmarks and Uncle had given her some additional monies. Most of these were spent with each day's stay in Helsinki. Her ticket funds from Richard were used to purchase her passage. This was going to be a real test of survival; what had she undertaken, she wondered? Was it the right choice?

An original postcard of the SS Cameronia.
Photo credit: Marxchivist from USA on Flickr

Finally departure time came and everyone eagerly boarded the connecting ship to England. "Sail on, speed away safely to America," shouted one of the youths. "Nopeasti, turvalisesti Ameriikkaan!" It was a two week long water crossing to England, and then a journey by land across England to Liverpool, where Senja would board the the Cameronia for America.

Senja was quickly settled into her bunk area. There would be a stop in the port of Turku before departure to Hull, England where they would arrive by February 22. This portion of her travel would be another sixteen day's journey. She was thankful she had a strong stomach as the ship rolled through the icy waters.

Senja would never see Finland again. Tears of longing for her family filled her eyes. "What have I done? I've left my family forever! In my haste I've broken the family bonds. Oh God, watch over all of them, and me, forever!"

With her head buried in her pillow, she fell asleep dreaming of a new life in America. Would she be happy with the choice she had made? Would Richard be a good man who would fulfill her dream of a prince charming? He was such a handsome man in the picture and he wrote so well. Only time would tell. She was off to a new world!

It was March 8, 1922 as the Cameronia steamed into New York Harbor. As immigrants, Senja and all her passenger acquaintances would have to pass inspection through the investigation lines of Ellis Island. She had heard so many stories of rejection, she was almost afraid to clear her throat or cough. She blinked her eyes to make sure there was nothing to obstruct her vision as she looked at signs on the walls instructing travelers where to go. "I don't want to have come this far and have to be sent back to Finland," she thought.

Standing tall, aware of inspectors along the walkway, Senja held her head high as she walked to the inspector's station. She had not been chalked by any of the observers on her way to the inspector's table and, after what was less than a minute's inspection, she passed! She moved on to the boat that would carry her across the last bit of sea to New

York. There, there would be a bus that would deliver her to the station where she should board a train for Painesville, Ohio. There were kind people who helped and directed her and other travelers. She felt like a sheep in some farmer's fold.

Ellis Island where new immigrants first passed before arriving to New York City. Here the original Finnish name of Lillbacka was Americanized to Lillback. Senja's name of Hautala remained unchanged at Ellis Island but would change to Lillback upon her marriage to Richard. Photo courtesy of National Park Service.

-11-
Onward from the Island

An average of five hours appeared to be the amount of time required for the standard visit to Ellis Island. Now for those who did not pass the physical inspection, it was 'Heartbreak Island.' They were marked with chalk by an observing inspector and found to be unacceptable for this new world. There were many who ended up weeping as they were led to a retaining area from which they would be sent back to their homeland.

However, there had been little for Senja to worry about as her health was fine and she was strong in body and mind. Not knowing English, she was communicating by friendly smiles, nodding her head to agree, shaking her head to disagree, or lifting her shoulders if she did not understand. It seemed to be working for her.

She needed to send a telegram to Richard Lillback to inform him that she would soon be in Painesville, Ohio. She showed the man at the ticket window Richard's address and the information he had sent her about which train she needed to ride. She was able to send a telegram informing him of her anticipated arrival in Painesville the next day. Many things could have gone wrong but everything was going well. She was thankful as she folded her hands in prayer.

New Life in Ohio

It was a long journey on the New York Central train as it sped across America's countryside. This America was really a big country and there were villages after villages, cities after cities, and farms that stretched for miles, with hundreds of cows and horses in large pasturelands. The mountain scenes were fabulous; she had never seen anything like them. The people on board were friendly and Senja smiled at them. She would say when they spoke to her, "Finland, America, Ohio." People would smile back, and they became friends. Her amiable personality had enabled her to make friends easily over the years. Now it was a very essential tool and it helped her overcome her anxieties.

Having dozed off many times, the travel distance was quickly closing in and she would soon be in Ohio. How soon would that be, she wondered? Had her telegraph message been delivered? Would Richard be there to meet her? Her thoughts began to race wildly as she considered the initial meeting. Would it be love at first sight, or would she hold off with formality for a time of getting to know Richard's personality? Perhaps he would not like what he saw when he met her for the first time. Well, at least she had made it to America, and she liked the country as she was seeing it.

It would be good to visit with Grandmother Wilhelmina and Aunt Hulda. It had been so many years ago that she had seen them. She was but a little girl of ten when grandmother had left for America. The talk in Alajalrvi was still about the big Crown wedding of Wilhelmina Karhula and Jacob Lillstrang on June 2, 1874. It was seven days of celebrating the wedding with dances and partying that included the whole village. There had been a lot of banqueting which involved the large wedding party of seven bridesmaids and seven groomsmen in their finest attire, including the village priest and other officials. Such an elaborate wedding seldom took place. Most weddings were usually on a smaller scale. Following the week's celebration, the bridal couple moved to Vimpeli, the home area of the Lillstrangs. The family grew and in 1905 they left Finland for America with three younger children, Jacob, Oscar and Hulda. Left behind were Johanna and Liisa, who mothered the Bergbacka side of the family.

Senja with Family. From left to right: Baby Visti, Maria Visti, Senja Lillback, Anna Lillstrang, Grandma Wilhelmina Lillstrang.

Will It Be Love?

Senja had observed her mother Johanna's sadness when her parents departed for America. Her mother's loneliness was compounded with the loss of her husband nine years later. Those were hard years emotionally for her mother. She had suffered birthing nine children and died at the age of 41. Senja, the oldest surviving child, had endured those difficult years. With her mother's death, she became the parent to her own brothers and sister. Mercifully, her aunt and uncle, the Hannulas, were nearby in Finland and took the children into their family. Uncle had even tried to bring about an honorable marriage match for Senja when he arranged her betrothal to the tailor. That probably would have been a very nice wedding. Well, this was America, she couldn't anticipate any great frivolities. She needed to be happy just to be here! Oh dear, what if she does not even like Richard?

With all these thoughts racing through her mind, she was reviewing past history as though she were flipping the pages of a photo album. She closed her eyes and breathed a prayer for direction and was soon fast asleep not realizing that she was only a few miles from her destination.

Suddenly she heard the conductor announcing as he passed through the railcar, "Painesville. Painesville, Ohio, next stop."

She knew that she had to move quickly to get off the train. This was it. Why had she let herself doze off at the very end of the trip? She reached for her bag and gathered everything together quickly. She had always been quick to move and now it paid off. As the train came to a screeching halt, she was up on her feet with her bags in hand. She was ready to jump down the stairs onto the unloading platform. There, at that precise moment, she saw the man she had come to see. In that moment she knew she did want to marry him. It was love at first sight!

Her blue eyes looked into his matching, twinkling blue eyes, and she trembled as his out-stretched hands reached for her as she descended from the train. "Welcome," he said. "I hope you had a good trip. I've been eagerly waiting for you. We'll catch the streetcar to Fairport. The grandparents are waiting for you there."

Getting Acquainted

The ride on the streetcar to Fairport was but a few miles. As they rode along, Richard spoke of Grandmother Wilhelmina and how happy she was that Senja was going to be here to stay. She had been preparing for this day.

The Lillstrang family had been increasing in number as their children Jaakko, Oskar, and Hulda had all married and were having children. Richard related that, on his coming to America in 1918, he found he had two sisters, Anna and Marian, and two brothers, Fredolph and Walfred, born to his stepmother Hulda, who was Senja's mother's sister. Explaining the family, Richard said to Senja, "When you marry me, you'll not only be my wife, but my legal aunt, also!" He began to chuckle as he related the close-knit relationship they would enjoy. (As the years increased, Isaac and Hulda added Rudolph, Everett, Harold, Ruth and Delores to the Lillback family.)

Senja enjoyed the twinkle in Richard's eyes as he made humorous conversation, and she was happy to be able to stretch her legs from the long train ride. The walk from the streetcar line on High Street to the house on Sixth Street was not a long one. Few people owned automobiles yet. Streetcars, horse-drawn buggies and wagons provided transportation in and out of the village. Richard was strong, and it was no effort for him to carry her baggage.

"Terve, tervetuloa! Welcome, welcome!" said grandmother and Aunt Hulda as they wrapped their arms around Senja in greeting. "It's so good you have come here to Fairport. You'll like it here. Life has been good here."

"What a lovely woman you have become," said grandmother. "You were but a child when we saw you last. Thank God you are here safely! Come and sit down and have some supper with us. We have been waiting. Was your trip a good one?"

Senja was hungry; it had been many hours since she had had a real meal. She began to partake of the feast of beef mojakkaa (stew), rice pudding with fruit soup, homemade bread and, of course, coffee with cardamom nisu coffee bread.

Grandfather Lillstrang welcomed her and commented on the increasing size of his family. The Lillstrang household was a busy one. Although their own children were gone, Richard's father, Isaac, and Hulda and their children lived with them. "Two together are better than one. They have a good reward for their labor," he said. "If they fall, the one will lift up the other, and they can keep each other warm. Richard, you've made a good choice bringing Senja here."

Richard made no comment, but he was anxious to show off the house he had purchased on Fifth Street to Senja. He was very proud of his two storied, three bedroom house. He felt it was very important that he establish his own home. Senja was also anxious to see it. What would it be like? Would it be as nice as that of the tailor's in Finland?

-15-
Richard Lillback

Richard, as a child, and his family in Finland.

It was late March and the courtship of Senja and Richard kept them busy getting to know each other's personalities and learning about their lives as orphans in Finland. Richard had been raised by his elderly Lillback grandparents and two maiden aunts. One aunt had enjoyed his rascally behaviors and the other aunt was very pietistic in her judgments and even discouraged him from playing his button accordion. She would hide the instrument and later, when the other friendly aunt would find it, it would be returned it to Richard and he would play again.

Through the months of April, May, June and July Senja and Richard went for daily walks most evenings around Fairport Harbor. Walking along the sandy beach of Lake Erie and watching the big steamships coming into the harbor bringing iron ore from Minnesota to the unloading docks on the Grand River was an exciting sight for Senja. There was a lot more going on here than the farm country in Alajarvi where she grew up. She decided she liked Fairport, but she was wondering daily how Richard measured up in her future life. He was not pushing for instant matrimony, and she wanted to get to know more about him, too. He worked during the day at the Diamond Alkali Company and was being trained as a plumber.

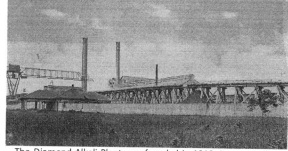

The Diamond Alkali Plant was founded in 1910. It grew to be a big industry in Fairport Harbor.

Richard enjoyed his work and spent his lunchtime entertaining his coworkers with humorous stories. Senja had taken a serving job at the local Poikatalo, a Finnish restaurant catering to people without famili es. Although Richard had proposed marriage by mail and had been friendly in courtship, he was very busy proving his ability to be a good provider and citizen to Senja.

Richard was also involved several evenings a week with five men reading and practicing the lines of a Finnish play that was going to be performed at various temperance halls in Ohio. He was also writing a monthly journal for one of the Finnish newspapers in Duluth, Minnesota under the byline of Riku. He had a talent for writing and reciting poetry. It was keeping him busy. Although his education in Finland had been limited to the basics offered in elementary school, he was extremely intelligent and especially skilled with words.

There were many young men who liked the saloons, and although liquor was illegal in Fairport, there were many speakeasies. Bootleggers plied their trade in the area. Kasvi Temperance Hall in Fairport had been organized early in the 1900s to help Finnish families abstain from alcohol. There were twenty-eight saloons scattered around Fairport providing for the thirsting habits of a multitude of single men. Richard's father Isaac was a member of the Temperance Hall. Richard was not a member, but he and his actors used the hall to present their plays.

The Temperance Hall in Fairport circa 1928. At this time, the McKinley School building had burned so school was being held at the Temperance Hall. Hulda and Isaac Lillback are pictured in the front left. The fourth adult from the left in the front is Wilhelmina, Hulda's mother and Senja's grandmother.

A Third Proposal

The Honorable
Mayor
of Fairport:
Dr. Amy Kaukonen
1921-1923

Richard kept busy with his work and his play performances. He was fascinated by Fairport's new mayor, Dr. Amy Kaukkonen, and her spirited fight against the liquor traffic. Richard upheld clean living and was ready to speak his piece in the campaign to elect Amy. The women of Fairport had been incited by the nondrinking men to cast their vote for a woman. Thereby Amy won the election for mayor, becoming the first woman mayor in Ohio. She began to boldly arrest and imprison illegal liquor sales people and bootleggers bringing in alcohol from Canada to Fairport.

One August evening before the election, Richard surprised Senja by saying coyly, "It's time we made a trip on the streetcar into Painesville. I've been so busy getting the play ready, and you have been getting too involved with your work. Let's take a trip Saturday and go watch the shoppers on Main Street in Painesville."

It was a nice day for the excursion to Painesville. "Let's get off the streetcar here at the city park and take a walk to one of those benches. It'll be cool under the big trees," said Richard. As they walked along, Richard suddenly stopped. Taking Senja by the arm, he led her to the bench under a big oak. "I've been waiting for the right place to properly ask you. Here it is, under this spreading oak tree. Will you be my wife?" Senja was astonished. She had been waiting for this question for the past months and had begun to think perhaps the marriage was not even going to happen.

"Oh, Richard," she said. "I thought you were never going to ask." She snuggled into his strong arms and he kissed her. He did not reveal that he was aware that she was probably waiting for the proposal. She had been playing it cool and was saving her money to repay him for sponsoring her voyage to America. However, she had not offered the money to him yet. She worked hard saving the money to cover her deep longing to be needed and loved. She did want to be loved by Richard.

"We can step over to the marriage license bureau across the street," Richard said as he whisked her up from the park bench. "I've spoken to Pastor Gabriel Lipsanen and we can be married next week at Suomi Zion Lutheran Church. I'll put a ring on your finger and let the whole world know you are mine! I love you."

The time of waiting had proved to Senja that she was happy to become Richard's wife. Working at the restaurant had revealed to her that she loved to serve and that she liked the company of people. She would do that in her home! It would be a place to refresh and entertain people around her kitchen table.

Suomi Zion Lutheran Church was a full Finnish congregation and had been established by early immigrants from Finland in the late nineteenth century. All the people spoke Finnish and the marriage ceremony on August 18, 1922 was performed in Finnish. "Oh, if only sister Aune could be here and brothers Reino and Tauno and Toivo and Uncle Nikolai," breathed Senja as she bowed her head in prayer. "Thank you God that you've made this possible. Please walk with us through life."

-17-
It's Official

The wedding was well attended with family and guests. Senja had already made many friends there in the community. She liked people and they were there to honor Richard's mail-order bride.

Richard kissed his love, and following the celebration of the wedding with cake, nisu and coffee, he took her to his home and, as he carried her over the threshold into the house at 507 Fifth Street where a "Just Married" sign hung on the front door, he said, "This is the fulfilling of my dreams, my dear Senja."

"Oh Richard, I love you, and I've loved this house from the first moment I saw it. Yes, Richard, this is where I want to be," she said. Senja was ready to be part of Richard's life, body, soul and spirit. And she would be a welcome and complementary part of the Fifth Street community of Fairport.

Richard and Senja's Wedding Photo

Who Came For Coffee?

Neighbors on Fifth Street came, one by one, carrying flowers and gifts for the newlyweds on the block. Richard had furnished the house with basic furniture. All of the gifts of dishes and linens, given by relatives and neighbors, were appreciated and quickly put into use. Senja's greeting to each one was "Welcome! Come in and I'll put on a pot of coffee." Some of the neighbors Senja became a friend to were: Iisakkila, Lurvey, Kallio, Katila, Liikaluomma, Hanninen, Rajamaki, Potti, Kytta, Pohto, Tompkins, and Anderson. Thus it went for several weeks; Senja's hospitality became well known on Fairport's Fifth Street.

Senja's Fairport Lady Friends (Senja on far right)

On Mondays the neighborhood ladies stopped midmorning for washday coffee at Senja's and on Tuesdays they took a break and left their ironing also to come for coffee. Soon it became the established time on those weekdays for the women of the neighborhood to drop their morning chores and assemble at Senja's for a pot of coffee. Senja was kept busy baking nisu bread to take care of her morning guests. Whatever went on in the neighborhood, especially births and deaths, was discussed and considered at the daily coffee times. The Potti brothers had established a funeral parlor across the street. Whenever these young men needed a woman's hand for mending garments, they would call on Senja.

One day one of Fairport's Finnish citizens died. The grieving family had the body taken to the older, established mortuary in Fairport. Senja was very upset and approached the grieving family and suggested that they have the body moved to Potti's for burial. "If we don't support the Potti Home, there'll be no Finnish establishment for our dead. You have to move your family member here to Fifth Street's Potti."

Ini Visti and Senja Lillback in Fairport Harbor

The family agreed and the body was moved. The Potti Home became the approved Finnish mortuary in Fairport and also in several other cities such as Ashtabula as well as Detroit as the establishment grew. Many years later, at the time of Senja's death, the Potti Brothers commemorated her with beautiful flower arrangements and gifts showing their appreciation for her early encouragement and kindnesses to them.

Kasvi Temperance Hall

Richard's casting of actors in his plays soon included Senja. She was always good for a character role, even if the play did not have that particular role written in it. It made the men perform more discreetly when she was present. Many of the rehearsals were carried on at their home, and of course, coffee was always served during the course of the evening. When the play was ready for presentation, it was performed at the local Fairport Kasvi Hall or the Plum Street Hall. They would perform also at Kilpi Temperance Hall in Conneaut and Sovinto Temperance Hall in Ashtabula.

Some of the three act plays they presented were: *Syden Kirous* (Reasons for the Curse) by Evald Jakku, a murder mystery, Henrik lbsen's *Yhteiskunan Pylvaat* (National Leaders) translated by Joel Lehtonen, *Savon Sydamessa* (In the Heart of Savo) by Martti Wuori, *Merkitty Mies* (The Marked Man) by Artturi Leinonen, and *Maaran Paassa* (At the End of the Road) by Arvi A. Seppala.

Actors in the play *Maaran Paasa* were H. Pihlaja as the chemist, Dr. Sanmarck; Senja Lillback as the mother of the chemist; Hilma Kallio as wife of the chemist; Esa Mietty as the artist painter, Aarne Kartio; Aili Viinikka as Jenny Kautto; Richard Lillback as doctor of Physiology; and H. Nuuija as Mili, the doctor's servant. This play was performed in 1931.

Some other local Finnish performers were, as listed in *Syden Kirous*: M.Lehti, Miss Hakli, Miss Wuori, Mr. Wuori, J. Maki, Marttila, Kenhola, and M. Lehto. These performances were under the direction of Richard. The actors' names are incomplete but listed as they were found marked on the two manuscripts.

A few months after the marriage, Richard and Senja became aware that by the following year in August of 1923 they would have a gift for which they had both hoped. Morning coffee times with the ladies sometimes were bypassed as morning nausea took preeminence. Play rehearsals continued, but Senja did not take an active part performing for a while. However, she faithfully provided coffee breaks for the others. She was dedicated to that role and now she was going to have an additional role to perform.

During those months of pregnancy, Senja and Richard often wondered what kind of child they were bringing into the world. As prospective parents they did not have the ability to know the genetics of what that child would be. He or she would be theirs to mold and teach in the growing years ahead, should God grant them those shaping years.

Life Takes a New Direction

The healthy birth of a child is the fulfillment of a happy mother's dream. Senja had witnessed the many births of her own siblings in Finland. She had also observed the deaths of some of these infants when her mother had joyfully birthed but later grieved their passing. Those had not been happy times and, as Senja anticipated the birth of her own child, she had many thoughts. They were thoughts filled with both good hopes and fears. "Oh dear Lord, if only this child will be healthy, I will do my best to teach him the right way of life," she prayed. And it was so: Eugene Richard was born a healthy child. He was a strong and alert baby, and papa Richard was proud of him. "He will fight for the issues of our Finnish people when he grows up. He'll be our spokesman when our strength is gone," Richard predicted.

Richard and Senja with Eugene at their home on Fifth Street. (Others pictured are unknown)

Senja had birthed a healthy, strong, male child. Little did she and Richard know, they had been given a child who would be able to easily spin and teach math formulas as if they were merely puzzles. He would also be a forceful leader on various sport fields and later lead British and American soldiers through dangerous mined battlefields in the Roer River area of Germany in World War II.

A year and a half later after Gene's birth, another son was born; he was christened Eino Armas. Again, the Lillbacks had been given another strong, healthy child that would grow up to be a sports leader, a creative builder, and a brave sailor who would attack the Germans as a Seabee at Normandy in 1943. He would also do battle on the Japanese front, helping make American freedom a lasting one.

When Gene was eighteen years old, Senja gave birth to her third son, Esco Edward. He was their love child and kept them active and alive as they aged. Esco was an athlete also, and, during the age of Elvis Presley and the Beatles, he entered the American army and served in Korea. During World War II Esco had given comfort and stability to Richard and Senja during those troubled war years. His childhood antics kept everyone laughing as he'd race around the house on his tricycle with his vocal motor "prr, prr, prr" resounding loudly.

The sons of Richard and Senja with their wives. From left to right: Esco, Ruth, Laurene, Eino, Eugene, and Elaine Lillback.

As Eugene and Eino were growing up, Senja loved to take the boys to Fairport's sandy beach where she could watch the children learn to swim, grow and mature. It was a good time to continue visiting with the neighborhood ladies and friends. Playing together, the children soon gathered around the spread tablecloth on the sandy beach, sharing their lunches and thermoses of coffee. Coffee was declared the tastiest out of the thermos at the beach!

-21-
Life with the Boys

Enrolled early in the Sunday School at Suomi Zion Church, the boys were introduced to the Aapinen, the basic Finnish ABC book. Every Finnish child would learn a little basic reading in Finnish as well as the Bible stories taught to them in Finnish. They learned not only to read and write Finnish, but were taught moral and spiritual life-giving principles.

The boys attended Fairport's McKinley School, often under the tutelage of Finnish teachers such as Alma Saari or Laina Somppi. They were learning to speak grammatical English as well as some Finnish through the instruction of these teachers. This was back in those days of freedom to speak several languages in the classroom.

Senja was happy also that she herself wasn't burdened with having to learn to speak English. She was comfortable hearing the firsthand Finnish reports about her boys from the teachers, friends and the children. She felt there was no need to learn English. It was great being Finnish in America. Senja also never changed her immigrant status by becoming an American citizen. She made her annual report to the United States government as a happy, honorable, Finnish immigrant.

A quiet lad, Eugene enjoyed school, always excelling in math and reading. Eino was also quick to learn. However, he enjoyed entertaining his classmates with a variety of antics that would cause his fellow classmates to break out in merry laughter. Taking hold of opportunities to amuse his fellow students, he would go up and down the aisles on his hands and knees when the teacher was busy at her desk. Senja was summoned into the classroom several times by the teachers and told of Eino's entertaining tactics. Years later, following a surgical procedure at the Painesville Lake East Hospital, Senja, on the eve of her death in May 1967, recalled those times as she shared with laughter those episodes with her three sons.

Eugene and Eino were the athletic duo of Fifth Street, and as they grew they became enamored by the Ohio State University football great, Esco Sarkkinen, from Fairport. They wanted to play great football, too, just like their hero. The boys, now in junior high school in Fairport, pleaded frequently with Richard, "Pappa, let's move to Painesville. They have a really good football team at Harvey High. We want to play ball there with those other Finnish kids, the Northenders of Painesville." It was a growing, conflicting issue.

-22-
Lillback Sporting Legacy

Richard had been involved playing the tuba in John F. Jacobson's band in Fairport. They practiced Wednesday evenings in the basement of the Plum Street School, and performed on summer Sunday afternoons in the Fairport Village Park. They were also involved with the Ashtabula Humina Band which eventually made an excellent performing trip to Finland. Richard, because of his work, was not able to participate in the band's trip to Europe.

Richard with his tuba.

Eugene had been offered a trumpet and lessons by Professor John Jacobson. His son's wife taught music to the children in Fairport Schools and his son Arvo went to New York City and played in the pit orchestra at Radio City. Eugene later regretted that he'd rejected a great opportunity of learning to play an instrument. He rather followed the sportsman's dream and played football and basketball, first for Harding and then later for Harvey High in Painesville.

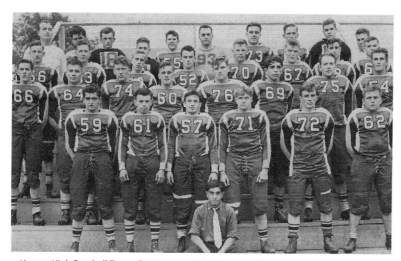

Harvey High Football Team. Eugene was #54. Eino was #71.

All three of the Lillback boys were members of Harvey High's football and basketball teams. Eugene and his brothers won many honors as they played many sports for the Red Raiders. Eugene was inducted into the Harvey High Hall of Fame on November 2, 2002. His son Larry Lillback made the presentation for Gene as his brother, Esco, grandson, Daniel, and other family members listened. Brother Eino who had refused a college football scholarship and entered the services of the nation during World War II was now sidelined by illness.

23

Harvey Basketball Champions from the 1940s. Eugene was #11.

All of Richard's brothers: Whitey, Lefty, Rudy and Harold, were born in Fairport and were sports enthusiasts. His dad, lsaac Richard III, loved, cheered for and played baseball. He was often called Casey for the baseball great Casey Stengel. His sons Whitey and Lefty were known for their keen eye on the ball and their ability to hit the ball for the Fairport teams.

Richard knew nothing about the rules of American sports since he grew up in Finland. However, he attended Harvey's football games and watched his boys play in the games. Not knowing the sport, he would laughingly relate how he'd stand when other observers stood and cheer when other Painesville folks cheered. He was, after all, a proud dad! Senja was proud, too, but she'd wait at home where the coffee pot was quickly boiled for whoever came calling after the game.

The Harvey Red Raiders were proud and thankful at the close of the 1941 football season. Three of the Finnish Painesville north-enders, sons of Diamond employees, had enabled the team to win the Lake Shore football championship. These boys were Don Luthanen, Eino Lillback and Eugene Lillback. Their dream had been fullfilled!

Following high school graduation in 1941, Eugene was approached by Coach Paul Brown to join Ohio State's freshman football team. Gene accepted this opportunity and enjoyed the experience of training and playing with Lou Groza, Dante Lavelle and other players who later joined Coach Paul Brown on the Cleveland Browns professional football team. The tale is told of the 1942 season games in which Gene ran 13 touchdowns as a freshman player. Older team members had been drafted into the country's service, and the freshmen were playing as starters for Ohio State!

-23-
In Service to their Country

After his football days, Gene enrolled in Reserved Officer Training. His time there was cut short when he was drafted into the United States Army. No longer was he training to be a medical doctor but was preparing to serve as a staff sergeant in the infantry. Senja, a blue star mother of World War II, related a soul-stirring story that occurred as she was awakened from sleep in the middle of the night. There at the foot of her bed, she saw

Eugene dressed in his army uniform. He did not speak, but she, overcome by stress, began to pour out her heart in prayer to God for the protection of both Gene and Eino and other servicemen. Sometime later, Senja received mail from Gene which told of a disastrous jeep episode.

Gene had been riding on the backside of an army jeep as his platoon advanced over German countryside. Wearying of the ride, Gene jumped off the jeep and began walking. The jeep, moving on ahead, suddenly hit a ground mine and exploded, killing all those riding in the vehicle. The letter now gave explanation to Senja's vision. Thankfully she continued in her prayers, not only for Gene and Eino, but for all servicemen.

Gene was awarded three medals for bravery that later became the parents' "show and reflect" items with guests at coffee times at home. One of two Silver Star designations read:

> On 23rd February 1945 when his platoon sergeant became a casualty near Ruhrdorf, during the assault crossing of the Roer River, Staff Sergeant Lillback unhesitatingly assumed command. Although intense enemy fire covered the area, he courageously led his men through mine fields towards the enemy positions. Skillfully deploying his men, he destroyed the emplacements with grenades and small arms fire and succeeded in killing or capturing the entire crew. The initiative and outstanding leadership displayed by Staff Sergeant Lillback enabled his company to continue its advance and reflect highest credit upon himself and the military service.

Eugene's Silver Star

The second Silver Star was awarded for the destruction of the German bunker which Eugene destroyed single handedly, saving the lives of both American and English soldiers.

The third medal awarded to Gene was Britain's highest award, the British Silver Medal of Honor. King George VI of England gave this for the destruction of a mined field and the enemy position. Many British soldiers were spared from death because of Gene's actions. The commendation read:

> ON 23rd of February, 1945 when his platoon sergeant became a casualty near Ruhrdorf, during the assault crossing of the Roer River, Sergeant Lillback unhesitatingly assumed command. Although intense enemy fire covered the area he courageously led his men through the mine fields towards the enemy positions. Skillfully deploying his men, he destroyed the emplacements with grenades and small arms fire, and succeeded in killing or capturing the entire crew. The initiative

and outstanding leadership displayed by Sergeant Lillback enabled his company to continue its advance and reflect the highest credit upon himself and the military service.

-24-
Wartime Stories

How different were Gene's informative letters from his brother Eino's who was in the midst of wartime hell? Not wishing to worry his folks, Eino had prepared and packaged many letters mailing them to arrive with regularity at home. The message was always the same: "Dear Mom and Dad, I hope you are well. I am fine. Your loving son, Bill." Eino had become known as Bill to his fellowmen, family and friends.

His many battlefronts included that of Normandy and the developing battles with the Japanese. Their fight was carried on at multiple points as they headed ever closer to Japan, island by island. Finally they arrived in Japan itself close to bombed-out Nagasaki which had been reduced to ashes by the atomic bomb. What honor was given to those brave young men as they faced the worst battle site of the ages! Can Americans be thankful enough for their sacrifices?

-25-
Cultural, Political and Religious Activities

While Richard and Senja's sons were spread all over the world during the war, their home and heritage was always in their hearts. The history of the Lillbacks in Finland is traced to Härmä. Today there is a Yläharmä and an Alahärmä, Finland, which was under Swedish rule for 600 years. They gave Finns Swedish names. The name Lillback had a Swedish origin, meaning "little hill over yonder." The red Lillback farmhouse still sits there on the hill from which various siblings moved to various surrounding areas. In times past the name has been changed to Lillbacka and even to Makinen, meaning "hilly." Isaac Richard III grew up in Untamala, Finland under the tutelage of his Grandparents, Isaac Richard II and Liisa Walli Lillback. He was given careful instruction in the religious training of the Lutheran Church.

Untamala was not far from the beautiful Ylistaro church. Its beauty motivated the esthetic senses of the whole community. It had not just one balcony, but a second level one also. Church functions and performances were well attended. Growing up in such a performance area, Richard began to use his creative skills to entertain his youthful friends in their gathering places. He learned to play the button accordion skillfully. He developed a comical routine which he performed for all his acquaintances. He was, according to childhood friends, quite a performer.

At eighteen, having received passage money from his father in America, this young man had taken the step of faith and come to Fairport, Ohio. Here he found that he could freely entertain his peers with his music, wit, plays and poetry. With his marriage to Senja, he had ascertained that she would make their home a place accepting visitors, a place for communication with others and a place for play rehearsals. After the boys were born, it was also a gathering place for the boys and their friends.

-26-
Finnish Speaking and Politics

Various speakers involved in the Finnish arts would write to inform Richard they were coming through the Cleveland area and would be available as a speaker if he could arrange a gathering.

Mr. Onni Syrjaniemi

Onni K. Syrjaniemi, a newspaper editor and lecturer for the Temperance movement, was a frequent Fairport speaker at the Kasvi Temperance Hall. He had a number of speeches that he freely offered around the United States that benefited Finnish causes. He had served as editor of a number of various Finnish newspapers in New York City; Fitchburg, Massachusetts; Cleveland, Ohio; Ashtabula, Ohio; and Duluth, Minnesota. Richard wrote news articles for Onni's newspapers and often performed poetry presentations at his meetings.

It was Onni Syrjaniemi who wrote to Richard in 1936 of the anticipated coming visit of Emil Hurja, private pollster of President Franklin D. Roosevelt, to the Ashtabula-Fairport, Ohio area. Everything was to be "at the ready" in Fairport for his coming. He was making a tour to Finnish areas to encourage local support of Roosevelt in his presidential campaign.

Hurja, a young Finnish news reporter from upper Michigan, had worked for the Democratic Party and was able to gather data on the political

27

behavior of Americans and systemize the information so that elections became accurately predicted. This helped lead to Roosevelt's ability to be elected to an unprecedented third term with power to authoritatively take over Washington.

Hurja enjoyed what he had wrought, but he began to regret the centralized government that had come about. Following Roosevelt's third election, Hurja broke with the party and became a Republican. He didn't, therefore, arrive for the meetings in Ohio, but there was at first, great excitement in anticipating his coming.

America's political scene was also wrapped up with the daily news of the Finnish-Russian Winter Wars of 1939-1941; the wars were stressing Finland's minimal resources. They didn't have the machinery or the manpower to fend off the Russians, but they fought brilliantly and bravely, thus saving their country's independence.

After the war, Finland, deeply indebted to America for war loans, quickly began to pay off her war debt to the United States. Recognizing this honest and determined attitude created a great spirit of honor in America whereby Finland was recognized not only for a hard fought battle, but also for their honest endeavor of paying their war loan, which was something other nations with war debts had not done.

During Finland's war with Russia, various American Church groups gathered together having social events to raise funds to help the plight of displaced Finns and orphans. Finland's people determinedly fought on every front, many losing their homes and loved ones. Whole communities from the Karelia area lost homes and livelihoods. They were displaced to other parts of Finland where they shared the homes of other Finns.

A typical story is that of a widowed Aunt Jenny Pyhtio who lost her home in Sortavala. She was displaced to Valkeakoski, with her mother Alexandra Tikka and Jenny's four children. While working for a factory there, she became very ill with typhoid fever. Graciously, the factory owners placed her under quarantine, providing her lodging and care in a special area of the factory until she was once again able to work to provide for her family.

-27-
Offering a Helping Hand

Congregants in American Finnish communities came together in many local areas to share the burden of their kinsmen in Finland. On a regular basis, Senja would cook the coffee at the Finnish Bethel Baptist Church in Painesville where the folks would sing and pray together on Friday nights. They closed the evening with coffee and fellowship; monies were collected at each meeting for Finnish war relief and to help orphan children.

Rev. Raymond Vargelin, from the Zion Lutheran Church, spearheaded the Fairport area drive among Finnish congregations.

Individuals also mailed packages of coffee, rice and sugar wrapped in clothing to relatives in Finland. Letters revealed the great encouragement the people received from these gifts. They helped keep up people's morale. Although it was still the Great Depression and it had been a time of economic downturn in the United States, Richard was able to work at the Diamond Alkali three days a week. Funds were low everywhere but packages to Finland were faithfully mailed to relatives and war orphans.

-28-
Riku Lillback

By this time Richard was recognized by his pen name of Riku. He would encourage the use of Richard by his family, but he used his craft name, Riku, when he wrote his stories and poetry and told his jokes. He liked his pseudonym; the name was catchy and fit his personality. The name Richard, a family held heritage name of honor, was far more appropriate as a middle name for his son Eugene.

"Riku Talking." Richard had an office in the basement of his Fifth Street home.

Richard "Riku" was often called upon to write poetic verse to memorialize various occasions such as weddings or funerals. One of the early Finnish family friends, Matt Kautiainen, passed away. Richard composed and recited the following verses in Finnish, which are translated here into English. The memorial poem read as follows:

"A REMEMBRANCE FOR MATT KAUTIANEN"
February 27, 1950
By Richard "Riku" Lillback
English translation by Elaine Lillback, English meter and rhyme by Peter Lillback

I bring praise to the Redeemer. A majestic hymn fills these halls.
I wouldn't change with another, for any other place at all.
Just days ago with finality, we met together at a home.
With joy I paid my earthly fees placed inside an envelope.
Brethren of Zion's congregation had February tenth as date.
At Matt and Maria's invitation, we joined them to celebrate.
During the program, Matt revealed how home and body wore away.
"Time's erosion can't be healed. I sink beneath my crown of gray."
"My life will soon be gone," he said. "I'll change my church and where I stay,"
"For a place where fees and debts will be stamped 'Forever paid.'"
With these words we sensed his loss. We felt his hope and knew his thoughts.
He meant Christ's death upon the cross. For Jesus paid salvation's cost.
Now we're standing in death's shadow. A filled grave will soon be closed.
Departure time has come with sorrow, and our hearts feel eternal woes.
But it seems the wind is bringing his greetings from far beyond:
"My loved ones, not tears but singing, since the cause for grief is gone."
"Fight on Mother. Fight on Youths. Soon your walk on earth is through."
Rewards are great. Your crowns are bright. Let past joys ever glow inside."

Painesville's Välikylä

The north end of Painesville City was known to the Finns as Välikylä, which translates as the "village in between." The Välikylä was composed of areas north of the railroads in Painesville City and the streets in between before crossing over the Grand River into Fairport. This included North State, North St. Clair, Sanford, Hine, Elm and Skinner Avenue. On these streets, particularly those such as Skinner, Elm and Hine, many of Fairport's younger Finnish families built their new homes.

It was a residential area composed mostly of Finnish American families. The Bill Katila family had established a successful corner grocery store on North State and Hine Avenue providing local shopping for residents. Bill, of early Fairport ancestry, and his wife, had established themselves with the Painesville Merchants. His brother Neal had a prior business in electronics in Fairport.

In the1940s, on the corner of North State and Skinner was Bethel, the Finnish Baptist Church built by Rev. Toivo Tervonen and his helpers. The church had been established in the 1930s in a storefront building on Fairport's High Street in the old Finn Hollow area.

There were other nationalities living in this area also. Included were Italians and Hungarians. The children of these families provided the athletes for Harvey High School. It was to a former sea captain's home on Skinner that Richard moved his family after selling their home in Fairport to the Wolf family.

A Friday Evening Church Group at the Sea Captain's House (1958)

This sea captain's house sat back at the end of a long driveway which went past the John Walli property. This was a long walk for the boys to Harvey High School, but they were happy with the challenge to play sports in Painesville. It also was the introduction to Tilda Walli who hired the boys to keep her large garden weeded. Evaluating their worth, she paid them in pennies, thoughtfully weighed out from her large penny jar collection.

While living in Fairport, Senja and Richard had befriended Reverend and Mrs. Victor Holopainen who had come to Fairport from Toronto, Canada to begin a Baptist work on High Street across from the Toubman Department Store. Finnish shopkeepers had operated a photography shop, a shoe store and a furniture shop there on the hill in these stores during the Finn Hollow days.

Rev. Victor Holopainen was an elegant revival preacher, stirring the hearts of the listeners. The storefront tabernacle was always filled with a variety of Fairport's Finnish residents. What he decided to do came as a big surprise to everyone: Richard had bought Victor an old automobile for five dollars and taught him how to drive it around Fairport. Within a year, Victor had purchased a brand new car in which he set off to explore the state of Minnesota. Here he later moved to take over a pastorate in Cloquet.

-30-
Bethel Baptist Church

One of the attendees of the Baptist Chapel was Mikko Pohto, the father of Dr. Allan Pohto, the dentist. Mikko would share his witness as a Christian believer singing the song "I Always Cast My Cares on the Lord" and follow it with his testimony of his personal faith.

Rev. and Mrs. Victor Holopainen, founding pastor of Bethel Baptist Church.

He had helped bring his eight Pohto siblings to Fairport over the years. Having never owned an automobile, he traveled to work at the nearby Diamond Alkali on his bicycle. Incredibly on a foggy day when returning home from work, his life was taken by an automobile driven by a visually handicapped driver in the fog. She ran into him on his bicycle and killed him. His faithful attendance was now over.

On Sundays, Rev. Holopainen elegantly played the violin and his wife accompanied him on the guitar as they sang many beautiful songs in the minor key. They had left persecution in Finland to escape to Canada and later Ohio. Their birth area was in Finland's Karelia, which was taken over by the Russians during Finland's Winter War of 1939-1940.

The work of the church grew into a determined Baptist congregation that began to search for and prepare their own church site. With so many of the Finnish families building homes in Painesville, it seemed that the most appropriate place to build their church was Valikyla, the Finnish village in north Painesville.

Rev. Holopainen was not a builder; he was a preacher and artist. With his return from his car trip to explore Minnesota, he suddenly announced that he'd been offered the itinerant pastorate of three congregations in the Palo, Aurora, and Cloquet, Minnesota area.

This unwanted news was a blow to the young congregation. The people were very sad; what would they do with this newly begun church? Would he leave them? Would they have to find another pastor? They were determined the church was to continue. With prayer they sought wisdom and they found another pastor, Rev. Toivo Tervonen from the Beverly Street Baptist Church in Toronto, Canada to come and resume the work begun by the Holopainen family.

Rev. Tervonen was willing to move to Fairport, Ohio and continue the fledgling work. He was also a gifted musician and a man unafraid of work. Thus it was that Rev. Toivo and Eva Tervonen, with their three children Anneli, Ulla, and Allan, were soon residents and citizens of the United States of America, pastoring the Finnish Baptists of Fairport. The Tervonens moved their family into the Välikyylä area on Skinner, and their home became a well-attended Sunday afternoon outdoor worship center.

Bethel Baptist Church Youth Group at the Tervonen Home on Skinner Avenue. From left to right, back row: Eugene Kaski, Carl Walli, Eugene Lillback; Row 2: Eloise Tikka, unidentified, Doris Wilberg, unidentified, Rev. Toivo Tervonen, Eva Tervonen, Ina Rinta, Elaine Tikka; Row 1: The Tervonen Children: Allan, Anneli, Ulla.

-31-
Rev. Toivo Tervonen

Rev. Toivo's Finnish background was from Finland's Swedish-Finnish eastern coast and archipelago. The couple was musically gifted and capable of speaking in Swedish, Finnish and English. Toivo, having the ability to design and construct, was the right man for building the church.

Toivo preached and following a 1939 Easter service he baptized nine new believers in a homemade baptismal tank at the Fairport church. It was his suggestion that the church find land and build in Välikylä. There was no Finnish church there, but there were a lot of Finnish people.

He had found it wise to move his family, now five, from Fairport to a larger home on Skinner. His residence became the site for many Sunday afternoon services. The neighbors came, and following the service his wife would serve coffee and Finnish pastries. It was not long before the congregation had purchased a lot on the corner of Skinner and State Streets to plant their church roots.

Digging a foundation began in earnest as Rev. Tervonen motivated the group to build a worship site. The Fairport church building served them for the following year until the wooden sanctuary in Painesville was fully completed. Rev. Tervonen not only designed the building and constructed it but, following its completion, he went on speaking tours in Michigan and Ohio to raise funds to help finance the ensuing costs. Services continued in the church, including a children's work. Vacation Bible School was conducted that year with sixteen children attending.

Bethel Baptist Church. From left to right, back row: Rev. Tervonen, Anneli Tervonen, Eloise Tikka, Marilyn Heleen; Front row: Ulla Tervonen, Gladys Wakkinen, Allan Tervonen, Arthur Sironen.

Sunday Fellowship

While yet in Fairport, Finnish people loved to stay after the service to visit with each other. Thus, many of the services were concluded with the serving of coffee. Senja, assisted by Maria Pohto, Hilda Heleen, Ida Rajamaki, and Pauliina Huhtanen prepared and served those who were present. The gigantic, gallon sized enamel coffee pots would be boiling on the gas stoves in the kitchen during the worship service. The four long tables in the dining area were set with coffee cups and saucers. Nisu and korppuja were always served with the coffee.

One Sunday, on Maria Pohto's birthday, Richard honored her with one of his poems at the coffee celebration. The translated poem follows:

"MRS. POHTO'S BIRTHDAY"
By Richard "Riku" Lillback
English translation by Elaine Lillback, English meter and rhyme by Peter Lillback

The October wind blew leaves down, swirling them along the ground.
Inside, a mother wrapped her babe as on her humble bed she laid.
Born in a cold hard Finnish world, the mother held her little girl,
"O dear child," were her words, "You're born into a chilly world."
"God of heaven, please bless my girl, born into this freezing world."

The mother wept and finally slept, with her babe warm on her breast.
After a long night, came new day. Her mother's prayer was still the same.
Many years have come and gone and mother isn't heard at dawn.
Beneath cold earth her mother sleeps. But her prayer, her girl still keeps.

The little baby is now grown with eleven children of her own.
Her life has reached an honored age, Sixty-eight on today's birthday.
Her award is one of joy: her garden blooms with girls and boys.
Here friends and children wish their best, hoping her life finds more success,

"Maria Pohto, blessings to you! In coming years, may this still be true!"
"May your health be the best, with much strength and happiness!"
How willing you've always been to sacrifice for your children.
If they come under sun or stars, they always find you working hard.

Some children sadly learn too late, their mother's love to appreciate.
How wonderful if in her life, they'd thank her for love's sacrifice!
So child, are you too late? Child, please don't hesitate.
What keeps you from speaking of the value of your mother's love?

It's not too late, there's time today to honor her with heartfelt praise.
Thank her now with this chance for her love shown in the past.
There's great comfort we can know that children can trust also,
That parents' selfless prayers above are answered by our Father's love.

Continuing Fellowship

Often on summer Sundays, Mike and Mary Lake would entertain the church group at their Rt. 86 home in Painesville. It was often a worship service and coffee time in their picnic hollow by the river. Finnish Midsummer Day, June 21, known as Juhannus, was celebrated there with a burning bonfire.

Another outdoor site was the John Tikka home on Shepard Road in Perry. It had a driveway around the grassy park, and made a wonderful place for a summertime meeting. Congregants enjoyed hearing the scripture read and singing the hymns in the park. Lempi Tikka would serve big pots of coffee, nisu and an iced cake.

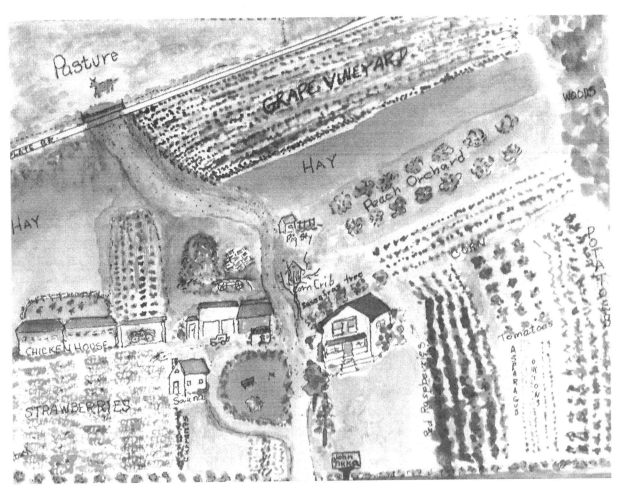

A watercolor drawing of the Tikka farm by Elaine Tikka Lillback

The Alex Sironen Family. From left to right, ront row: Selma Sironen, Walter Rinta, Maria Sironen, Alex Sironen, Mary Sironen; Back row: John and Ilmi Rinta, Lempi Sironen, Matilda Walli.

At the John Rinta home on South Dayton Road in Madison, it was fun to sit on the old platform swing made by grandfather Alex Sironen who had farmed there in 1915. It had served many generations of Finnish children and adults. Many Fairporters loved to drive out to the farms on Sunday afternoons, enjoying the fresh air, fruits and vegetables and, of course, drinking and sharing the fresh coffee! Aunt Ilmi always had a nice cake and nisu to go with the coffee.

Mike Lake was a wonderful host. He had been trained as a butler in wealthy Cleveland homes. When his wife spoke, he jumped to it and served people extremely well. When the weather was cooler, and friends were inside their home, it was all more formal. One could observe the culture being polished up among the Finnish people. On warm days, they would entertain in their outdoor home down on the river level.

The Reverend's wife, Eva Tervonen, became ill and had to be hospitalized for tuberculosis. At first she was treated at Painesville's Lake County hospital, but later moved to Denver, Colorado where her treatment consisted of fresh air and bed rest. That was before antibiotic medicine had been made available and cures were almost unknown. Toivo brought a niece of Eva's, Miriam Beck, from Minnesota to stay with the children. The congregation carried on with the work of the gospel.

Rev. Toivo Tervonen with his wife, Eva, and their children, Anneli and Ula.

Rev. Toivo Tervonen with his second wife, Helena.

A few years later, following the death of Eva, Toivo married Helena Rajala from Toronto, a well educated, musically gifted helpmate. Their work continued on in Painesville for several years. With missionary spirit and evangelistic enthusiasm, Toivo and Helena were drawn to Minnesota to encourage Finnish believers in church ministries in Chisholm and also in the Thunder Bay area of Canada through a weekly radio ministry and traveling evangelistic services. They were able to establish a church in the Intola, Canada area bringing together believers that had been nurtured by women missionaries in Ontario.

A west coast pastor by the name of Juntunen was the next to serve the Bethel Baptist Church in Painesville. He was skilled in both the English and Finnish languages. This family continued the good work in Painesville for several years.

The Juntunen Family

-34-
Finnish Missionaries and Ministry

Rev. Topias Vainonen, a Finnish Baptist pastor from Inkeri, Russia, had escaped Communist rule in Russia by crawling under a barbed wire fence. He found freedom in Finland. Later in life, he became the pastor of the Intola Baptist Church in Ontario, Canada. He had previously come to Toronto to the Bay Street Baptist Church where he'd served as a pastor of the Finnish congregation for several years. During his time there, he married Alli and they had two boys, Daniel and Donald, and one daughter, Astrid. The daughter is married and lives now in Toronto, Canada. The boys are located in various places in the United States. They received their education in Painesville, Ohio's Huntington School.

A Finnish Canadian Baptist missionary, Esther Risanen, had been serving as a missionary among the Finns in Port Arthur and its outlying communities for a number of years. She was very capable in speaking, teaching and serving people fearlessly in all kinds of weather. Snowshoes and skis were part of her equipment. She had a wonderful way with children in teaching them handwork.

For the summers of 1943-1946, she requested Elaine Tikka from the Fairport-Painesville area of Ohio to serve with her in the teaching and music ministry in the Thunder Bay area. Esther was among the women missionaries that had prepared the community to build the large Intola church with Rev. Toivo Tervonen.

Rev. Tobias Vainonen with his Canadian hostess, Esther Rissanen, and Elaine Tikka.

Some years after pastoring in Toronto, Rev. Vainonen moved with his wife and three children to the Bethel Baptist Church in Painesville, Ohio. Here he served faithfully for many years until the church was transferred to the Ohio Baptist Conference. It had served in providing the Finnish people a place for their weekly praise and worship services. This was after the Finnish Winter War of 1939-1940 and America's battle in World War II.

During the Korean War and the Vietnam War, the congregation ministered through Sunday School classes to the English community. They also provided Vacation Bible School during the summers to neighborhood children. The local congregation supported Ken and Irma Wheeler in their twelve years of missionary work in Barbados, West Indies.

During one of the Wheeler's yearlong furloughs after four years with Berean Missions, they served the local church with a ministry to the English-speaking community. The Wheelers took over the ministry of the church at that time, living in the parsonage. When they returned to Barbados a year later, the Vainonens returned to the parsonage and to the work.

The Wheeler Family. From left to right, front row: David, Ken, Irma, Kendra; back row: Kenneth, Beverly, Phyllis.

The young people from the congregation serving in the United States army and navy during WWII included the following : Donald Lakia, George Visti, Ero Visti, Aini Visti (nurse), Eino Lillback, Eugene Lillback, Esco Lillback, Walter Rinta, Arvi Rinta, Henry Wanska, and Richard Wanska. The prayers of the people helped to preserve the lives of these soldiers, enabling them all to return safely home. No serviceman from the church was killed during those years of conflict. God had answered the prayers of this congregation.

-35-
Finnish Lutheran Church and School

Huntington Elementary Sunday School

Besides the Baptist group in Painesville, there were the Lutherans from Fairport that had Vacation Bible school in the summer time and Sunday school time during the school year at Huntington Elementary School. This school has now been destroyed and is now a memorial park for children to play in. Some of the children who attended the school (as identified by Lillian Cambpell from California) are: Albert Hervy, June Anala, Arnold Herpy, Josie Honkola, Margaret Honkola, Joan Katila, Helmi Nieminen, Lillian Nieminen, Gladys Annala, Jacqueline Katila, Gloria Myllykoski, Edwin Hyppa, Ralph Myllykoski, Onni Nieminen, Doris Tenkku, Nancy Tenkku. Teachers that served, but not pictured, were Esther Annala, Alice Matson, Elvira Concoby, and Anna Nieminen. Praise the Lord for their picture taken by Ann Nieminen on her little black camera.

Special Friends That Came to Visit

Probably this often-recited creed of elderly folk could have been Senja's declaration of her daily ministries to those who came to her door over the years.

"The more you give, the more you get:
The more you laugh, the less you fret:
The more you live abundantly,
The more of everything you share,
The more you'll always have to spare:
The more you love, the more you'll find
That life is good and friends are kind:
Not only what you give away
Enriches you from day to day!"

At the Lillback's Storr Street Home. From left to right: Richard, baby Larry, Eugene, Esco, Senja, and Lempi Tikka.

The most cherished and frequently received guests at Richard and Senja's home were their children and later their grandchildren. Eino married and he and his wife Laurene made their home with Richard and Senja when Laurene found it necessary to go to work. Grandmother Senja babysat two-year-old David, who began to learn Finnish. When Laurene would come home from a day's work, David would greet her with the Finnish words he'd learned: "Anna minulle vetta." Laurene didn't understand he was asking for water. "What are you saying?" she'd ask. Soon Laurene began to learn some Finnish through David, too.

One evening when Eugene and Eino were working, Elaine Tikki, who had married Eugene, left their first son, Larry, in Grandpa Richard's care. Elaine, Senja, and Laurene then went to a party. While they were gone, Grandpa Richard put his son's childhood boxing gloves on 4-year-old David and 3-year-old Larry. Then he sat back observing what he called a "lesson in self-defense." Larry relates now in his adult years that his grandpa prepared him at this early age to aggressively take the punches of life as they came to him. One could presume David found this to be true for him also.

When he had been living in Fairport, Richard had often thought that by moving to Painesville he would reduce the cost of Senja's coffee times; there would be fewer guests to treat. However, in moving to Painesville's north end, their home was on the bus-line from Fairport. It was very convenient for friends to take the bus to visit Senja at her Storrs Street home, stopping off at the bus stop near their house. It was indeed, a very convenient location!

The Lillback's Storr Street Home

One lady, Molly, who could argue court cases like an attorney, was a frequent guest. She would challenge other visitors as the devil's advocate, taking the opposite side of whatever issue was being discussed at the time. It could make for a heated discussion. One day after work when Laurene came to pick up David, she heard loud talking and thought Senja's guests were fighting. The debate, of course, had to be completed before Laurene was informed that the afternoon's outcome was a legal type, verbal conflict-- a challenging discussion, not a fight but all for fun. It was peaceful ending!

-37-
Senja's Close Friendships

Then there was *Pikku Toivo*, Little Toivo. He came faithfully every other week for Senja's coffee and for a haircut. Richard had been exchanging hair-cutting services with Toivo for many years. The interesting thing was that when Senja passed away, Toivo didn't come anymore. Richard had to find himself a new barber. Toivo apparently liked the coffee shop friendship more than the barbershop!

A young family with three children made weekly visits. Senja would always save her pennies for the children and have candy bars and gum to share with the boys. Bigger gifts such as a large doll were occasional gifts to the little girl. This friendship went on faithfully for many years. Once again, after Senja's death, the visits no longer took place, nor was Richard welcomed to their home. Somehow his hand hadn't brewed those special cups of coffee. These are the sad sides of wonderful friendships that suddenly ended.

Tilda, another special friend of Senja, was a former neighbor from Skinner Avenue. She would shop the grocery stores for food bargains, such as day old bread and fruits. She would visit her choice people and share her thrifty purchases with them. One day Senja informed the family that there was going to be a surprise 80th leap year birthday party for Tilda at her home. Guests were invited to come and present a birthday message for the celebrant. Tilda's house was filled with guests. Tilda's friends got the table ready for the birthday cake, the sandwiches and coffee breads. The dining room table was covered with Tilda's spread-out newspapers. The ladies were going to roll up the papers and replace them with a nice cloth for the special occassion.

41

"Oh no, not a cloth, just put fresh newspaper over the top of the other papers!" advised Tilda. So the party continued with much merriment but no special deocrations! "Happy birthday, Tilda!"

Some months later, Senja notified Elaine, Eugene's wife, that she needed to go and visit Tilda. She was very ill at home. Tilda had never been to the hospital in her 87 years so it was unusual for her to be sick. She was lying on the sofa in her living room with her legs swollen with water. Elaine questioned her regarding her health and inquired if she could do anything to help Tilda. The elderly woman shook her head. Elaine recited the 23rd Psalm and prayed that God would help Tilda in her illness. That night, Tilda was taken to the hospital where she died of kidney failure.

An unusual report came back a few days later when Tilda's sisters-in-law were at her house cleaning; they had finally unrolled the newspapers off of Tilda's dining room table. To their surprise, they found American dollars lacing the papers: twenties, tens and fives. They had almost thrown the money away with all the newspapers! Thousands of dollars were also found under the sofa cushions on which she had been lying that day Elaine had been to pray with her. Tilda had saved her first Finnish markka and many American dollars, but she couldn't take them with her when she died!

-38-
Close Family Friends

One of the nicest visitors that came to visit Senja and Richard was the Jack Saari family. As a bachelor Jack would love to joke and tell stories with Richard. One day he said, "I'm going to Finland to find myself a wife." Richard thought he was just telling a tale, but some time later, Jack came knocking on the Lillback's door with his new wife Bertha and their lovely baby girl named Ailiin.

What a fun day that was to see what Jack had accomplished in Finland! During the following years of the family friendship, the Saari family increased to three girls, Ailiin, Mary and Helen. Jack built his family a nice brick home with a sauna which the Lillbacks frequented.

The Lillbacks attended a house warming for the Saaris and Richard "Riku" presented the following poem in Finnish as a gift.

"THE SAARI HOME DEDICATION"
By Richard "Riku" Lillback
English translation by Elaine Lillback, English meter and rhyme by Peter Lillback

Jack and Bertha, you once schemed, an imagination, a sweet dream,
Of a new home with walls of bricks, a floor of wood you'd also pick.
Could this dream one day come true? Was it a yearning you couldn't do?
Would it be warm with inspiration? Could it meet your expectations?
Your dream at last took command and before long, work began.
With joy, friends came with tools to build, and soon your dream would be fulfilled.
How lovely is a home that's warm, a shelter from winter winds and storms.
It calms the restless seas of life, daily bringing strength inside.
With great labor and much strength, your dream home was built at length.
Each piece of lumber is well known. Each carefully cut and honed.
Countless nails have pierced the walls, binding it tight, so it won't fall.
A peaceful hint of love's built in, that soothes your blessed home within.
Expense alone can't build strong homes, then they're cold without love's songs.
Rich owners may even end their lives in sad despair and suicide.
So Jack and Bertha, now we wish you, that God's blessings will be with you.
May your home know happiness, for you and yours, peace and calmness,
Until the last beat of the heart, when one of you someday departs.
May Jesus comfort you inside, then with prayer trust Him as your guide.

Time Spent with Family

There were always guests at Richard and Senja's. Every day included a faithful stop from Elaine with her boys, Larry, Peter and Douglas. The children loved Senja's mojakkaa, riisi puuroa with strawberries, homemade oatmeal bread, nisu, and the whip cream they could squirt out of the canister over their dish of ice cream. It was always fun to visit. Senja spoke in Finnish with the children, but Richard spoke English with them. Those were joyful times; there was always a warm welcome, and the coffee pot was always ready to be served.

57 Newell Street

There seldom was a day when visits were not extended back and forth. On Saturdays Senja and Richard would come to visit Gene and Elaine's children at 57 Newell Street. They came also to 10487 Johnnycake when Gene moved his family there in 1960. Senja would bring with her five pounds of good ground sirloin beef and buns for making hamburgers. Elaine would get the grilling going and lunch was soon ready and served at the cheerful kitchen table. Oh yes, there was coffee for the adults, milk for the children.

When Gene changed his profession from YMCA group work and recreation to teaching math, he was extended a teaching and basketball coaching contract at North Baltimore, Ohio. Gene reorganized his family and his parent's lives by moving Richard and Senja to 57 Newell and Elaine and his children to North Baltimore, Ohio.

Eugene, Elaine, and baby Larry

It was a surprise move for Richard and Senja, and they most graciously accepted the new change of address at 57 Newell. Now, once again, Senja had a new location for her coffee house! They enjoyed that change in their lives.

Eugene's family also had a surprise move. They had a new opportunity for Gene's advance education in math a few years later at the University of Tennesse through the Jennings Foundation of Kirtland. The grant took them to Knoxville, Tennesee. Later, following several years of teaching and coaching football at Kirtland High School after the further Masters program, Gene returned his family to Ohio and began his years teaching as a math professor for Kent State University on the Ashtabula campus.

Another guest, a faithful visitor and neighbor of the Lillbacks from Elm Street, was Varma Kanyuh. She was the only daughter of Pauline and Gustave Huhtanen. Her father was one of the Finn Hollow dockworkers and her mother was the country rug weaver and former hostess of the Kasvi Temperance Hall on Eagle Street in Fairport.

Mr. and Mrs. Huhtanen with Varma

They'd lived in the Sironen boarding house in earlier days, and Mrs. Huhtanen helped make the coffee at the Fairport location of the beginning Baptist Church. Many of the gathered articles of Pauline and Varma are a part of the Finn Hollow display at the Finnish Heritage Museum today.

Varma married John Kanyuh who served as a railroad engineer with the Baltimore and Ohio Railroad Company after service in World War I. They never had any children. Senja held a 25th wedding anniversary party for the Kanyuh's in 1952. Senja collected twenty-five cents from every invited guest and a group gift of silverware and other gifts were given. Both sides of Elm Street were filled with parked cars as guests gathered for the party. Cakes, nisu and coffee were served of course!

Richard had decided to purchase some nearby property with acreage when land became available on Elm Street. It was a seven-acre piece of rich farmland. He purchased a nice tractor and began to turn over the soil and plant seeds; he watched them grow into lovely vegetables. In time he shared the land with others who desired to have a garden also. Eugene and Elaine's boys were getting big and needed a lot of food, so they planted a large garden with many kinds of vegetable seeds. In some time, they had lots of vegetables, including squash and pumpkin! It was an exciting time and a time of great vegetable give away. An unknown neighbor was a daily take-awayer with her bushel basket full of a free harvest of zucchini squash!

Lillback's Home at 535 Elm Street.

During the following years, the little garage-house that Richard established at 565 Elm had not only housed them, but had given a start to many young married couples. Eino and Laurene Lillback, Enid and Uno Esselstrom, Dick and Candy Wanska, Harold and Katherine Lillback, Esco and Ruth Lillback, Elaine and Eugene Lillback and Larry and Miriam

Lillback all were young tenants in their time. The soil was rich and wonderful for not only growing fruits and vegetables but also children. Today there is the beautiful elementary school at that location, Elm Street Elementary housing many children.

-41-
Changes for the Family

Those early years of visits with Richard and Senja were wonderful years for Gene and Elaine. They had come north from Columbus, and as they lived in their home on Elm Street, they decided they needed an extra room. Gene laid out the plan, and they added a master bedroom. During that time, Elaine went to the hospital to give birth to Peter. It was a hot, muggy June night, and she became one of many expectant moms waiting for delivery on the evening of June 9th. Later that month, Elaine's sister Eloise gave birth to Jim. The babies grew up together with many happenings. The families did so many things together

Lillback's Elm Street House around April 1953. The addition had just been completed. Pictured: Elaine with sons Larry and Peter.

that the babies soon became good, mischievous friends. Years later, it was a sad day in Jim's eighth grade that he found that he had to have surgery for a tumor growing on his brain. After many cranial surgeries and many months in the Cleveland Clinic, Jim was released from the hospital. His life has been a wonderful testimony of God's gracious goodness to Jim and the woman he eventually married, Nadine.

At the archeological dig in the late 1970s.

Ancient bones were discovered out in the soil of Gene and Elaine's home, and Chardon's elementary students led by an English professor, Dave Emery, of Kent State University performed an archeological dig. A written report was made in the Ohio Archeological magazine. The bones were judged to be an old tribe of some thousands of years' precedence which had occupied the area. Today the property has passed on to the Painesville City Board of Education, and a beautiful elementary school has been built on this land. It is interesting that this land has become a monument of all those who walked there in the many past years.

46

Probably the most important part of the story to unfold of Senja, who came to be a giver to so many in America, is now to be shared. It was a regular day, and Elaine had a phone call from Senja. "Elaine, who is a doctor that I could go see? I have been vomiting all morning, and it is black."

Elaine rushed to Senja and took her to the Painesville hospital emergency room where she was treated by the caring doctor. Senja was ordered to have surgery for a strangled hernia. Senja had acquired the hernia from tending to a run-away milk cow during her pregnancy with Esco in 1941. It had now, twenty-six years later, strangulated. Dr. Downing was assigned as the physician to care for her. He called Elaine into his examination room to show her the melon-sized hernia. "I have never seen one so large," he said.

"Nor have I," Elaine replied. With these remarks, Senja was rolled away into surgery. Senja's boys came to visit her later that day. She was very sharp, recalling episodes of son Eino's mischief as a child in first grade. They were all enjoying her recollections. They spent a good visit with Senja and everything seemed to be all right.

By early morning Senja had suffered a stroke. Lingering through the day until shortly after midnight hours in a coma, her long needed surgery for the large six inch naval hernia had taken its toll. It was but a matter of time until she would be gone. The boys began their vigil and late that night Senja passed away into the world she had been looking for, into heaven's glory. The family was very sad.

-42-
Remembering Senja

Senja's Funeral. From left to right: Richard, Eugene, Eino, and Esco at the Potti funeral home.

There were lots of flowers. Flowers came from so many people, and from the Akron Potti brother who remembered Senja's help getting them started as a mortuary many long years ago.

Senja came with a mind to serve, and so she did, with Richard: they served many cups of coffee. It was a sign of their friendship and it brought everyone to remember the common bond they had as Finns. On that day of her illness, John and Lempi Tikka had come to visit Senja. Thank you Senja and Richard. You have done well your job of a living friendship. God bless.

47

The Lillback and Tikka families had met in the Fairport Harbor Finnish Baptist church many years before. They had become friends not knowing that, eventually, their children would join their families through the marriage of Elaine and Eugene. Below is a poem Richard wrote to remember his good friend and the father of his daughter-in-law.

"IN MEMORY OF JOHN TIKKA"
Oct. 16, 1960
By Richard "Riku" Lillback
English translation by Elaine Lillback, English meter and rhyme by Peter Lillback

Run, run, my special friend, for so your story once began.
You leapt from tent to mat for sleep, like a moose by mountain peaks.

Those thoughts again were renewed, when the airport came in view.
Soon up from the ground you flew, as the plane pierced skies of blue.

Helpless man learns at length, he cannot rule wind's mighty strength,
Settle down, trust the plane, you're safe over clouds and rain.

The realm below with sun so bright, soon disappears as if at night.
Then clouds, like giant drifts of snow, shine around with brilliant glow.

The wind's breath helped lift you there as skies changed with moving air.
Your racing hearts made thoughts soar, by pounding, beating even more.

Over Georgia on this flight, you witnessed a majestic sight.
The sun rose with colored rays, peeking over dark clouds' haze.

The ground was black, no light in sight, darkness reigned the whole worldwide.
Yet for you, the sun was beaming, indeed, sunrays were brightly streaming.

That panorama did amaze, you'd not forget it, all your days.
"Let there be light, and there was light." God's Word doesn't deceive like night.

So thoughts traveled out to space, where human things are out of place.
Jesus only holds us there. For future skies, we must prepare.

With honor your trip was made. Thanks to God you flew that way.
"Come and visit," a couple said, "Enjoy Florida's sun instead!"

Now we thank the Lord who's great. Creation is His vast estate.
Slow and weak John flew and ran, yet fast he leapt to God's right hand.

The Finnish Heritage Museum

There was a good bit of discussion regarding the formation of a Finnish museum group to honor the Finnish ancestry of the Fairport Harbor Finns such as Richard and Senja. Principled leaders were talking about this. Among those were the following people: Linda Katila, Veikko Malkamaki and a committee. Elaine Lillback heard firsthand about Linda's desire to have a Finnish red farmhouse museum somewhere in the Fairport area. Elaine's cousin, Aili Hakojarvi, had related Linda's wish to her. Linda was a retired teacher and a retired elementary school principal in the area. Veikko was a Finland native who was doing home exterior and interior painting and home decorating.

On November 18, 2002 the group, Ailiin Andrews, Vivian Heikkinen, Linda Katila, Raili and Matti Lehtonen, Laura and Veikko Malkamaki, Niles Oinonen, John Ollila, and Viola Pohto, met to discuss the formation of a Finnish museum. The next meeting was announced for January 13, 2003 at the home of Linda Katila on Mentor Avenue in Painesville, Ohio.

Elaine's friend, Ailiin Saari, invited her to the museum meeting at Linda Katila's home. Elaine was happy to accept the invitation to the second gathering of people interested in the founding of a Finnish museum group. Those attending the meeting were Veikko Malkamaki, Ailiin Andrews, Elaine Lillback, John Ollila, and Linda Katila.

As a group, they discussed the type of society they wished to form. Linda related her dream of the red Finnish farmhouse. The group contemplated what type of membership they would have, the cost of membership, and the name for the organization. Eventually the name, Finnish Heritage Museum, was chosen at a later meeting. Officers were elected. They were: President, John Ollila with Linda Katila as supporting president; Elaine Lillback, Vice President; Ailiin Andrews, Secretary; and Veikko Malkamaki, treasurer.

With these officers the group went forward for one year, meeting at first in the old Senior Fairport Center. When that building was to be disposed of, they moved to the new Senior Citizens' Center building on Fairport's East Street. They met there for a number of meetings, electing new officers.

Honoring Finnish Heritage

During this time, the group grew from a dozen people to fifty folks. They had, through the good work of Ailiin Andrews and Laura Malkamaki and others, presented beautiful displays of Finnish items in the Fairport Library, the McCrone department store window on Second, and a beautiful Finnish exhibit at the old Lake County Historical Society in Kirtland, Ohio. These displays were meticulously set up giving acknowledgement to Finnish design and authorship, making for important recognition of Finnish art and music.

Plans were made by Laura Malkamaki and Ailiin Andrews, and under the Museum Director, Professor Emeritus Gene Kangas, to have a textile exhibit at the Willoughby School of Fine Arts on November 7th through December 17th, 2004. Also the Christmas celebration was to be held on Sunday, December 12, 2004 in the Harding High School auditorium. For this there was a special program honoring Finnish history and the functioning of the museum. Refreshments were served, memorializing the remembrance of sharing foods together.

Furthering the Society

The group talked about moving their society back into the old senior center. They had previously been meeting at Fairport Ohio's former fire station. They requested a grant from the United States government for $20,000 to improve the building and use it for twenty years. Since the old structure was in need of crucial repairs, the group had been meeting in the library Community Room. After several months, word came that the group had been approved to care for the old building that belonged to the Fairport Citizenry.

The Finnish Heritage Museum in Fairport Harbor, Ohio.

The president, architect "Henry" Heikki Penttila, had drawn up beautiful plans that were approved. Men were hired and work began. All of their plans and dreams were finally coming to pass and the old fire station was reborn. Remodeling began with the government grant of $20,000. These funds covered most of the improvement expenses.

By the second year of the group's existence, they had elected Heikki Penttila as president, Pat Spivak as vice president, Linda Kangas as secretary, Veikko Malkamaki as treasurer, Kathy Pierce as curator, and Lasse Hiltunen as webmaster.

-46-
Finnish Migration

It was a long journey for Finnish people to arrive in Ohio. Finns had come to Titusville, Pennsylvania in 1871 to build the railroad to Youngstown, Ohio. By 1872 some of these workers had come to Chardon, Ohio to help lay the railroad to Fairport Harbor. They brought their families and wrote to their friends in Vaasa Povince, Finland to come to help with Fairport's shipping docks.

Historically, by the late 1800s, there were around 200 Finns in Fairport Village. This included Finn Hollow where they had built houses on temporary dock sites on High Street. As time went on, the Finns moved these houses and established them in Fairport Harbor. These homes are marked with a commemorative marker today.

Later, other Finns moved into the outlying villages of Painesville, Perry, Madison, Chardon, Willoughby, and other communities. It is common to say that Finns are found everywhere.

Painesville provided the closest point, and an area that was known as "Valikyla" soon had many Finns on the various streets of Elm, North State Street, Hine Avenue, and North St. Clair. It was just next door to Fairport, a small bus ride away.

A Day of Celebration

Many years later, after all of the initial migration and Finnish establishment, it was time to celebrate the formation of the society in a building of their own. Many wonderful things had been happening so they could have a day of celebration. Heikki had announced that the building could be opened and the women came with their buckets, soap and rags for scrubbing. They worked late into the night so that ancient dirt was washed away. They founders could open the building the next day for the announced celebration!

Photograph by Lasse Hiltunen.

It was with great joy that they were able to welcome many friends and visitors to the gathering. The society had worked together to get the building ready and they had a program to present in the adjacent village park. How excited they all were.

First on the program outdoors at 10:00 a.m. was the story of Finn Hollow, presented by Elaine Lillback as her mother, Lempi Sironen, had related it to her many years before. The day went along with Finnish music and choral groups, and then, there was food prepared for the guests. It was a wonderful day and everyone had a marvelous time.

A group of folk dancers from Toronto, Ontario, called the Toronto Sisu Folk Dancers, proudly passed along their Finnish heritage and cultural values. Their steps and colors in Fairport Harbor showed as brightly as they do at home in Canada.

There was a special speaker for the evening, Dr. Patricia Book, the Vice President of Regional Development at Kent State University. Her academic discipline is medical anthropology. She told about all her grandparents that had come from Finland and made life possible for her.

Special museum musical guests for the banquet were Melvin Hakola, Professor Emeritus from Baldwin-Wallace College; Timo Lehtonen, clarinetist, son of George and Kaarina Lehtonen; and Rachel Ward, viola player, daughter of Roger and Bonnie Ward of Maumee, Ohio. Heikki Perttu, a local composer and arranger, joined with Hilkka Helena, an accomplished singer, born in Helsinki but now living in Florida. There were also the Pelimannit who performed as accompanists. The Finnish group of The Stubborn Finns, a singing group, also performed.

All in all, it was a most wonderful two days of programs. Everything was done so well; it is to be remembered as God's blessing on the Finnish museum and the bringing of people together. Other activities at the museum such as Finn Funn Fest were also well attended.

-48-
The Museum Prospers

Other enjoyable activities have happened at the museum over the years. On May 15, 2010, the community celebrated its first Finn Hollow Day program at the Finnish Luther Center on High Street. The celebration of John Morton, the Finnish American founding father and the last delegate to sign the Declaration of Independence, was honored by historian and writer of American history, Dr. A. Lillback, grandson of Richard and Senja, from Philadelphia, Pennsylvania. He has been acknowledged for his research and writing of *George Washington's Sacred Fire*. It became a number 1 bestseller in the United States. He gave an interesting talk about the early history of the Finns coming to America.

Dr. Peter A. Lillback at the National Constitution Center with an eagle carved from the wood of America's last Liberty Tree.

Following the presentation of the moved house plaques to the honorees of Finn Hollow Houses, attendees were happy to hear Fairport's Mayor Frank Sarosy declare that May 15th will henceforth be continually honored as "Finn Hollow Day" in Fairport Harbor, Ohio. That was truly exciting.

Many wonderful things have happened at the museum. Lasse Hiltunen has performed as Webmaster of their online presence which operates with the following address: www.FinnishHeritageMuseum.org. He collects the messages of the monthly museum speakers which are presented on the second Monday of the month at the group meetings. Most of the articles are interesting informational talks presented by the local people. Other local activities have been written about and posted also in the museum's files. Reports of interest come in from around the world. Visitors have been coming into the museum from the all over the globe.

Exhibits at the Museum

Bill Maki's daughter, Linda, passed away at only 50 years old. She had been gifted in music and as an artist on the harp. Bill made a donation to the museum to have the back room of the museum for displaying his daughter's achievements. There is a cabinet filled with her Finnish harps and costumes and other equipment. Her music continues as patrons look at her life's exhibit.

A carpenter, Isaac (Vilpakka) Willbeck by the trade of homebuilding, left all of his tools in lovely collection order and they have been contributed to the museum in his memory. He was a great builder and his memorable tool set is monumental when we realize the great works he created. Fairport has a notable collection of old, well built homes.

A Norseman, Leif Owren, fighting as a ski trooper in the 1939 War in Finland, wore his totally white leather uniform and helped Finland to keep her independence from the Russians. His white winter coat and other great trophies are exhibited in one of the glass cases. Lief's son, Michael J. Owren, Ph.D, a psychology professor from the University of Georgia, made the donation.

David Mackey, a wood working artist, had on display at the museum two of the many horses he carved out of basswood. He has made and painted these beautiful horses for his grandchild to ride. They are like the beauties of the merry-go-round riding circle. It is amazing what lovely things can be created in this life.

There are other trophies like the old weaving that sits in the gallery, on which Rebecca Steinback weaves almost every Saturday. She has created rugs, tablecloths and doilies. She is a certified weaver and began giving lessons in 2012.

Finland is famous for its weaving, and it is great to have the old loom of Kylikki Lehtonen redone by John Steinback. It is in good harmony in its use by Rebecca Steinback. The loom was made for Kylikki as a young girl to learn on in Finland, and after years of service it was in need of repair. It was fixed and preserved with John's great care.

The loom in The Finnish Heritage Museum.

Donations to the Museum

A wall hanging in the museum

Many artifacts, including pictures, books and relics of the past, have been gathered under the organizing and watchful care of Kathy Pierce and Suzanne Jokela. With local help, these women have created wonderful displays. Additionally, Larry LaBotta has carved out a five string dulcimer from the wood of the old table from the Suonio Bakery. His wife Janine aided him. Volunteer aid has been the life of the museum.

Elaine Lillback has contributed and lent many display materials from the Finn Hollow times. Those homes, still existing and historically marked, tell a great part about early Fairport. The money for preparing the house markers was paid for by a grant applied for by Laura Malkamaki. Each Finn Hollow House has the original owner's home name, giving recognition to the original owner of the home.

Some of the costume dresses of Finland are shown and displayed at the museum as well. An authentic copy of an original dress from the time of the Crusades has been donated by Mrs. Albert Helsius. It is from Tuukalan's Burial Ground near Mikkeli, Finland which was unearthed in 1886. It was sent to Mrs. Helsius in 1941-42 by the Finnish Embassy.

At the museum's early beginnings, the directors decided to vote annually and honor people, some living and some dead, who have contributed to Finnish history. Over the years the museum has added the following people to its Hall of Fame: Kai Haaskivi, 1955-), Zacharias Topelius (1818-1898), Linda Evelyn Hyppa Katila (1919-2007), Akseli Gallen-Kallela (1865-1931), Raymond W. Wargelin (1911-2003), Lillian Luthanen Robinson (1911-1993), Johan Julius Christian Sibelius (1865-1957), Eliel Gottlieb Saarinen (1873-1950), Bernhard Hillila (1919-2006), Paavo Johannes Nurmi (1897-1973), Mikael Agricola (1510-1557), Veikko Malkamaki, John Morton (1724-1777), Lasse Viren (1949-), Eila Hiltunen (1922-2003), Tarja Kaarina Halonen (1943-), Carl Wilhelm, Ville

The Wall of Fame at the museum

Vallgren (1855-1940), Johan Vilhelm Snellman (1806-1881), Elias Lonnrot (1802-1884), Elaine Tikka Lillback (1924-   ), Martti Ahtisaari (1937-   ), Urho Kaleva Kekkonen (1909-1986), Robert "Bob" W. Selvala (1934-2000), Kreeta Haapasala (1813-1893), Eero Saarinen (1910-1961), Rev. Dr. Gustav Axel Aho (1897-1973), Carl Gustav Mannerhiem (1867-1951), Saul Olin, and Jorma Lillback. Heikki Penttila matted and framed pictures of these elected people to the museum walls.

-51-
Connections through the Museum

Interesting people have come by to visit. Among these were Canadians David and Barbara Wainikka, an electronics specialist and a genealogist on a work/vacation tour. While working in the museum, Elaine Lillback began to hear about Thunder Bay, Canada. It was fascinating when she heard the name of Esther Rissanen mentioned. Elaine interrupted the Wainikka's conversation to find that they knew, in a warm, close relationship, this lady who had been a special workfellow and friend of Elaine's back in the summers of 1943-1946 in Port Arthur, Canada. Elaine had been sent to serve as a summer missionary among the Finnish people there. She had aided Esther in her summer work among Finnish Canadians in Ontario. The museum was making connections and reuniting old friends!

Barbara Wainikka was shocked to find someone in America who had been in her neighborhood when she was a little child. She and Elaine had a wonderful conversation and Barbara promised to send her a small self-written book of the life of Esther, called *Use My Skis, Lord!* Esther had retired in British Columbia in 1976 and has now passed on. The book she wrote covered a small communication about part of her life. The copy of her book is now located in the museum's library.

A Parting Tale

The plaque Elaine Tikka gave to Eugene Lillback in 1946 on the event of his wedding. Elaine and Gene were later married on April 19, 1948.

An interesting story to close this tale of Finnish resilience, connection, and prosperity is that of our author, Elaine, and her husband, Eugene Lillback. Back in 1946 as Elaine was visiting at a Sunday afternoon gathering at Mike Lake's home in Painesville, she was surprised to see Eugene Lillback who had come from out of town to pick up his parents. Elaine had purchased and wrapped a wedding gift for Eugene and his new bride, and Elaine was able to give it to him at this summer outing. Eugene was pleasantly surprised and thanked her for the gift. "Love Never Fails" was the theme of the gift plaque Elaine had given the newlyweds. It had the Bible verse John 3:16, "For God so loved the world that He gave His only begotten Son, that whosoever believes in Him shall not perish, but have everlasting life."

The following year, Elaine was stunned to hear that the returned soldier and former Ohio State football athlete had been rejected and his marriage was over. He was the son of Senja and Richard Lillback: They had always been held in honor. Gene had served in the United States Army in World War II and had been awarded two American silver star medals of honor for bravery plus a silver peace medal for bravery from the King of England. This was unbelievable for everyone to behold! How could he be rejected?

As time went on, it was arranged that Eugene and Elaine would go out for coffee together. Later, as their relationship progressed, Elaine discovered that the only gift Eugene had saved from his earlier marriage was the plaque she had given to him that summer Sunday. The Bible verse had real meaning for him and he had cherished the plaque! This plaque has hung on the wall of the Lillback house ever since and is still there until this day.

The Esselstrom Wedding, 1942. Eugene and Elaine were both members of the wedding party in this celebration. Little did they know that they would be getting married themselves in the years to come. Pictured from left to right: Eugene Lillback, Irma Tikka, Enid Heleen Esselstrom, Uno Esselstrom, Elaine Tikka, Arnold Heleen.

-53-
The Author's Ending Thoughts

What can be said now, all these years later? Gene and I had been married 38 years when the Lord chose to take him home. He had gone back to college to finish his degree after our marriage and then on to teaching and further math education. He really enjoyed his teaching. God honored him and gave him three sons, and we are proud of each of them and the work they are each doing. Life is not easy. We are to do that which pleases God. There are blessings despite the hard words that come and confront us. My life's helper passed away twenty-five years ago of lymphoma at the Cleveland Clinic. He fought the cancer through three hard years of chemo, radiation, finally yielding to the trial of a critical experimental bone marrow transplant.

That year there were 100 of these trials. It was critical, and the treatments were all very hard. He was a brave soldier and fought his illness to the very bitter end. I am sure there is a reward on the other side, another silver star for him for that.

His mom and dad, Senja and Richard, who came for coffee, were proud of Gene, and I'm sure that together in glory, they are proud of all of us Finns in Fairport and Painesville. If they could, they would join us for another cup of coffee. That is what we are all still here for! We have all come for that coffee that brings each one of us together.

This was the moment Elaine remembers seeing Eugene (far right) for the first time. He would have been around twelve years old.

58031294R00038

Made in the USA
Middletown, DE
18 December 2017